SALOM RIZK WAS BORN in 1909 in a tiny poverty-stricken town in Syria. Although he grew up as a Syrian, when Rizk was twelve years old he discovered that his mother had been an American citizen and that he could claim American citizenship. Two brothers and an uncle in Iowa paid his passage to the United States, but he arrived in this country penniless, homeless, and with no knowledge of our language. The story of his incredible experience in self-education and his rise to one of the most sought-after and inspirational speakers on American lecture platforms is contained in SYRIAN YANKEE.

There is an almost Biblical simplicity about the opening chapters of Mr. Rizk's story. These deal with the little Syrian town where he lived in a tiny hut with his grandmother and their sheep and chickens. Eventually he becomes a swineherd and attends a little Arabic school, where he discovers his American citizenship. The schoolmaster writes to his relatives in Iowa, who forward the passage money, but he waits five years in Beirut until his identity is finally established. After his arrival in America, Rizk enjoys a variety of employments; during the depression he conceives the idea of free shoe repairing for the poor, which spreads all over the country. In an amazingly short time he becomes a high-school pupil and later begins his career of lecturing under the auspices of the *Reader's Digest*. And the story he tells is always the same one—the story of a true American who made his way by courage and perseverance.

SYRIAN YANKEE

BY *Salom Rizk*

DOUBLEDAY & COMPANY, INC., GARDEN CITY, N. Y.,

To

THE REV. HAROLD E. SCHMIDT
without whose inspiring friendship,
constant encouragements, and help
there could have been no
Syrian Yankee.

Foreword

THIS IS THE stirring story of a little orphan vagabond who discovered at fourteen that his American mother had been visiting relatives in Syria when he was born, and that he was therefore an American citizen. Salom Rizk did not know a word of English when he left his war-impoverished birthplace to make his own personal discovery of twentieth-century United States.

Three years after his arrival in this country, having had only a few weeks of schooling and having earned his own livelihood, he was invited by the Rotary Club of Ames, Iowa, to make his first appearance as a public speaker. He discussed with moving conviction the unbelievable opportunities, and freedom, and fullness of life that he found here in contrast to the bare existence that was inevitable in his Old World home.

When Salom concluded his speech, his audience arose

spontaneously and there was prolonged applause, as there has been since in over a thousand auditoriums. But it was not the personal triumph that made Salom proud; it was the hope that a little bit of his debt as a citizen of this great land had been repaid. With characteristic modesty he knew that they were not applauding him. "They were applauding America," he said, "the land where this could happen to anyone."

Members of the editorial staff of The Reader's Digest first heard Salom Rizk in April 1939, when Lowell Thomas introduced him to the New York Advertising Club as the "Syrian Yankee." By now Salom was devoting full time to lecturing on "The Americanization of an American," and we were convinced that he had an important message, particularly for the youth of the United States.

During the 1930's, high school and college discussion was so focused on correcting the faults of democracy that the advantages of the American way of life were seldom mentioned. Salom's talk, wherever heard, produced a dramatically quickened appreciation.

As a public service, The Reader's Digest offered him to the high schools of the United States. He has since told the strange tale, which is here expanded into a book, to over 1,012,000 boys and girls in 1495 schools.

Superintendents, principals and students have written us hundreds of letters saying that Salom's passionately sincere talk was the most inspiring they had ever heard. A sentence from Father Flanagan of Boys Town, Nebraska, is typical: "Salom Rizk has made my homeless boys proud of being Americans."

With our entry into the war, Salom's personal tribute to the privilege of being a citizen of these United States assumed added significance. It was obvious that his autobiography would have particular timeliness and value.

Syrian Yankee is Salom's own story—a record of his adventures and of what America did to one immigrant boy, told in his own way. After reading it one exclaims, "Well done, Salom. We, too, thank God for a land where this could happen."

DeWitt Wallace

Contents

Syrian Yankee

CHAPTER I

Kbashy the Magnificent

NEARLY ALL THE THINGS that happened when I was a boy, in the places beyond our hills—in Lebanon and Palestine and Turkey, and in the far places over the sea—I didn't know anything about or even dimly suspect because we had no books or newspapers in our village. Most of the talk in our valley was the little talk of little people trying to scratch a living out of a mean and niggardly earth and trying somehow to save enough from the landlords and tax collectors and thieves to scrape through from one year to another. The little news that reached us came on the wings of rumor and hearsay, and so everything that was ugly was uglier and everything that was beautiful was more beautiful by the time we heard it.

There was oppression in the land, and suffering and gnashing of teeth. There were the people, as there are in every land, who took tribute of the earth, who gathered in the taxes and lived off the fat of the land, who had the power to say what shall and what shall not be done and who shall and who shall not do it; who gave the people stones and scorpions when they asked for bread, and who would not and seemingly could not understand that other men were like them. And there were the people, as there are in every land, who could not and would not stand it any longer, and they were always in a state of revolt, getting together in secret bands and writing and speaking and agitating and organizing for freedom; men who hid from the other people in cities and in caves; who fought back with the sword when they could against the cruelty and selfishness of those in power. But, as I said, I did not know anything about that then. Sometimes, though, our little village felt the harsh, bitter breath of the big storms that blew beyond the gray confines of our Syrian hills. Sometimes in strange and mixed-up ways they blew into our valleys and upset the lives of people in our village and in our homes. Then it was that we needed a peacemaker and a wise and gifted storyteller such as my grandmother Kbashy was.

One day, when we children were playing in the court in front of my grandmother's old stone house, a horseman came galloping down the trail that winds across the floor of the valley into Ybose. That was always a sight to fill us with wonder and excitement—a horse and rider clopping down the valley, rising and falling together with a single movement, dust rolling from the heels, tail flowing on the wind, breast and bridle ornaments flashing brightly in the sun. Sometimes we would prance around the village on willow branches, pretending to be as wild and pretty as Shikry and his beautiful horse. For this man, we soon saw, was Shikry, one of two Turkish tax collectors who lived in our village; the other one was his brother Tufik. Shikry was the older of the two, who had come recently from Kurdistan to take charge of tax collections and assessments in the district. A very handsome fellow he was, with his curled black mustaches and all his fighting things: the gleaming cartridge belts crisscrossing his magnificent chest, the jewel-studded dagger handle sticking out of a scabbard on one hip and the inlaid-ivory revolver butt surmounting a holster on the other. You couldn't help admiring him— when you were a little boy.

Shikry lived with his three or four wives in a house on the edge of the village. Now he pulled his horse up before the door, swung out of the saddle, and disappeared into his home.

It must have been half an hour later when we were startled from our play by a noise as loud as the bellow of an ox. It came from Shikry's house, and we looked up just in time to see him leap out of the doorway into his saddle like a huge cat. He was cursing prodigiously.

We saw a yellow boot go up and then flash down along the belly of his mare, burying spurs into soft flanks. The poor horse let out a scream, stood up on her hind legs and pawed the air as if a devil had gotten into her. She whirled, came down snorting, and stretched out into a mad gallop before our popping eyes. Just as suddenly she stopped and slid on all fours almost into the very door of the house right behind ours.

The village had been expecting something like this for two days, but when it happened it was as if we had not had the faintest hint of it beforehand, it all came about so suddenly.

Shikry's brother Tufik lived in that house with his wife Miriam. Miriam had excited the envy and jealousy of the women almost from the day Tufik brought her home as a bride. She was from near Beirut, a very pretty woman with a fine, light skin and city ways. Her clothes were very elegant—Frangy, or Frenchy, people called them, because they were like the French fashions in Beirut.

Some of the women had their suspicions about Miriam. For one thing, she was suspected of being a Christian. There was nothing wrong with that. But she was married to a Mohammedan, and if she really was a Christian, her marriage was made in hell. Of such a woman the Mohammedans said, "She is an untouchable slut who aspires to a place beyond her reach," and the Christians countered with

the saying, "The ewe in heat has left the fold for a wolf."
Miriam was banned by both sides, and she knew it.

For almost a week now her husband, Tufik, had been
away, over in the Jededah valley on official business. During his absence a strange man dressed in city clothes (they
were Frenchy, too) had visited Miriam. Right out in full
sight of everybody Miriam and the stranger had embraced
and gone arm in arm into the house. The whole village
was scandalized.

Two days the man stayed, and for two days the excited
women speculated about him and that woman. They could
imagine only one thing with enough logic in it to account
for Miriam's seductive clothes, strange manner, and disturbing aloofness. Quite plainly the stranger was one of
Miriam's past lovers taking advantage of Tufik's absence.

The stranger had departed that morning, while the
women peeked curiously and with increasing speculation
from doors and windows, gathering afterwards at the water
fountain to piece out the story.

That noon Shikry rode in and heard the scandalous
thing from his wives. Now he sat fiercely astride his danc-
ing steed at the door of his brother's house. His face was
livid with rage, and his mustaches seemed to curl even
more fiercely under the vehemence of his words.

"By Allah, may your bones bleach in the desert like a
dead camel's!" he roared, and the words clapped on the

wind like thunder. "If my brother does not tear you in pieces and feed your filthy flesh to the wolves, I shall shoot him like a dog—shoot him like an accursed dog," he repeated.

With that he whirled his horse around, whipped out his pistol and emptied it with a plumping sound into the body of an old dog resting lazily in the shade of our house.

Some of the children ran for cover, but I was petrified, rooted to the spot, and I remember praying, whether silently or not I cannot say, "O God, kill him before he kills me."

That august Personage, however, must have been busy at the time in other parts of Syria, because when I opened my eyes Shikry was still there, looking more terrible than ever.

With a final, punctuating gesture of contempt he spat upon the door, gouged his horse with his spurs, and sailed out of the valley in the direction of Jededah. Disdaining the trail, he struck across the fields, leaping stone fences and scattering chickens and goats as he went.

We knew what his mission was. Tufik was somewhere in the Jededah. The worst was yet to come; everybody could feel it coming.

The home of Tufik showed no signs of life. For all we knew, it was deserted, but no one made any attempt to find out. It stood there in the white glare of the sun, isolated, suddenly removed from the company of the other houses, stood there like a place marked for destruction. Judgment was upon it, and I watched it with a fear and foreboding as personal as death. I guess it was what happened to the dog that made me feel that way.

It was late afternoon. In the house Kbashy, bedfast from an accident, was telling me a story, more, I suspect, to divert my mind from the expected tragedy than from any desire to entertain me. Suddenly we heard the sound of running feet outside; then a shadow darkened the door. It was Miriam. Her eyes were wild and red with weeping. With a muffled sob she ran across the room and fell across the foot of Kbashy's bed.

It is hard to describe the scene which followed. Kbashy spoke words of comfort and courage to her and somehow managed to pull her together enough to draw out her story. It wasn't anything like the gossip. Indeed, it was wonderful, and when Kbashy told her so and made her believe it, Miriam's face was beautiful again.

But not for long. Pretty soon there was the clopping of a horse on the trail. Miriam's eyes grew wide with alarm. I held my breath and could feel my heart pounding in my breast. Kbashy spoke a reassuring word and smoothed the covers on her bed.

When he entered the village someone must have told Tufik where his wife was, because he came straight to our house. We could hear him dismount outside. He was putting tremendous energy into showing how he felt, and you could sense that the whole village was listening. He charged across the court like a mad bull, breathing profanity like fire. In the doorway he stopped. In one hand was a gun, in the other a whip. The only thing I could think of was the way Shikry had shot that dog.

But in that moment, in the doorway, an amazing change took place. It was a time-honored, ironclad custom of the Arabic world that did it. Once you cross the threshold of a man's home, the law of hospitality decrees conduct becoming an honored and beloved guest. Tufik put the gun into his holster.

"Salom, bring Tufik Effendi a drink of water," my grandmother said.

I jumped at the unexpected command, obeying as if pushed by an invisible hand. I felt Tufik's eyes on me all the while. I brought the water in a *kalai* and timidly offered it to him.

"Drink, Tufik; you are very thirsty," said Kbashy.

He hesitated a little, then took the cup from my trembling hands, and in just about three awesome gulps drained the vessel dry and gave it back to me.

"*Henia wa sachtein,*" my grandmother said as he drank; "double health to you, my light."

"Double health to you," he said to me. "May we drink

to your everlasting happiness at your wedding and may your noble grandmother live to look on and rejoice."

This was the extravagant, overstuffed language of formal gratitude—beautiful, very beautiful and touching, when things are right. But now things were not right, and you couldn't tell how much trouble it covered up.

"Sit you down, Tufik; you are tired," my grandmother said, "and we have much to talk about."

"You mean *I* have much to talk about," he said as he looked at Miriam.

"Yes, Tufik, you have much to talk about. We all have much to talk about—because others have talked too much."

"What do you mean?"

"I mean that busy tongues make tall tales, and tall tales make great tribulation."

"Tell me what you mean," said Tufik, glowering.

"Tufik Effendi, you must remember hearing a story about a king who lost his kingdom because he listened to idle gossip and believed it. Let me tell you that story. It is good to think about now."

Then, as if by magic, the room was gone and Kbashy was gone and we were in the court of a king. Our simple little peasant hut became a royal palace. Yet Kbashy was there, and in her eyes and face and hands we saw the people pass, the pompous diplomats and wise-looking counselors, the malicious gossips, the credulous old king, the angry people and the indignant queen. Breathlessly we followed the story to the very end.

And then we came back to the room; Miriam sitting there at the head of the bed, beautiful in the fading light; Tufik humped on his stool, his knees sticking up like a little boy's; I sitting on the floor, still in the spell of the story. You would never have guessed we had just been witnessing a drama in the court of a king.

After a pause Kbashy said, "Tufik, like that foolish old king, you have been the victim of idle tongues. Miriam is innocent of these rumors which you have been led to believe."

"But what about the man in my house? There was a man. Shikry——"

"Yes," Kbashy interrupted quietly, "there was a man in your house. The man was Miriam's brother."

"Miriam's brother!" he said, astonished. "I didn't know she had a brother. Why didn't you tell me you had a brother?"

Miriam sat up, startled. "I—I was afraid to."

"Why were you afraid to?"

"I—I thought he was dead."

"Why should you be afraid to tell me he was dead? Is death a disgrace?"

"I mean, I didn't think it made any difference if he was dead."

"Miriam is upset, Tufik," Kbashy interrupted. "She cannot tell it to you now the way she told it to me. Let me tell you. Until he came here Miriam did think her brother was dead. You see, when the Turkish soldiers raided her village, they killed her father and mother—the Lord have mercy on their souls—and Miriam and her brother escaped. But Miriam did not know that. She thought her brother was killed, too. By Allah's mercy he was saved and is alive and well. Miriam has seen him again with her own eyes. Of all their family they have only each other left."

"But why does he leave the same day he knows I am coming home?"

"Tufik, you must understand this. We cannot blame Miriam for what her brother does. Maybe we shouldn't blame him too much, either. He is a very bitter man. We must think how we would feel if the soldiers killed our parents. He thinks the government is bad. He hates it. He is plotting against it, and they have a reward for him. He is hiding from the officials, and you know you are an official."

"How do I know this is the truth? Maybe you are only making a fool of me. It is all a lie."

"Show him the picture, Miriam."

Miriam drew from the folds of her dress a piece of paper with the picture of a man and some printing on it. Tufik studied it a long time, it seemed, and then he exploded.

"A traitor to the government and you hide him? Why didn't you keep him here? Don't you know that is your duty? Don't you know you are just as guilty as he if you hide him? Suppose the officers find out he was in my home. Suppose they find out his sister is my wife. What do you think they will do to me? By Allah, we must find him. You must tell me where he is!"

"I cannot betray him," Miriam said, so softly we could hardly hear it.

"You cannot——" Tufik looked as if his head would explode.

"I cannot betray him any more than I could betray you," said Miriam.

"A faithful sister makes a faithful wife," said Kbashy.

Tufik looked at the picture on the piece of paper. "How do I know this is a picture of your brother? I never saw him. This could be anybody."

"Show it to the neighbors," Kbashy said gently.

"The neighbors!" Tufik barked.

"Yes, the neighbors; they saw him."

There was a long pause. Then Tufik said, "Come, Miriam, we are going home."

Tufik went out, and Miriam followed him. He stomped across the court, and I breathed with deep relief as he roared an extravagant threat to exterminate the whole village if any more idle tongues touched his doorstep with filthy rumor.

After a moment Kbashy's head fell back tiredly against the pillow. Then she turned her twinkling eyes on me and said: "Take good note, Salom, for seven days there will be no gossip in this village."

That's the way my grandmother was: she understood human nature; she was shrewd, wise, and practical; a magnificent teller of tales; a great and good woman. People in our village called her *umelsulch*, which means peacemaker. They took their troubles to her because she could always help. They trusted her because of the sweetness and beauty of her spirit: they said, "Our tongues cannot move without speaking her praise."

To her I owe my very life, and to her I owe the story I have to tell. For without her I might never have lived to tell it, or having lived, might never have stumbled upon the strange destiny Providence had prepared for me.

I wonder, if I were an artist, just how I would paint my grandmother Kbashy's portrait. Perhaps, to do her justice and to bring out the two things in her life which impressed and influenced me most, I should have to paint two pictures: one of the stories she told, the other of that story which she was determined not to tell. For there was a secret about me which she meant to keep as long as she could—because she meant to keep me. Not that she would have succeeded; at least I don't think she would have. But you never know about those things, and it still bothers me to think of what might have happened to me, or rather what might not have happened, had she been successful. About this secret—more in a later chapter.

My grandmother was born of a Christian Orthodox family in the little Syrian city of Rasheiya, which lies in a spur of hills off the northwestern slopes of Mount Hermon. They called her Kbashy because just below the hair line on her forehead was a mole which resembled a ripe blackberry. When she was five years old her parents moved north to Ain Arab, where she grew up and married. After a few years she and my grandfather went to the tiny village of Ybose, which lies at the bottom of a mountain at the upper end of an obscure valley in a region known as the Jededah. Here they raised three sons. And here they made their living working a patch of barren, stony soil on the estate of the local bey, or pasha as he was sometimes called. He was one of the many petty feudal lords who own the scattered bits of cultivated land of eastern Syria.

Partly because of her gifts as a storyteller, partly because of her skill as a cook and baker, my grandmother soon won the favor of the pasha, who was in the habit of bestowing rather lavish entertainment on his frequent guests. This was especially true when the tax collectors came to count the animals, inspect the woodlands, or make the grain collections; then the pasha counted on a good table to soften the Turkish heart and reduce the levies. When the tax collectors came Kbashy was always summoned to the castle—though it was really much less than a castle—to plan and prepare the feast

Then, I can well imagine, she was in her second element. The pasha's larder was well supplied, and she could cook richly, much more richly than in her own home. Oils and spices, fruits and vegetables, sheep and goat and fowl, plenty of fuel, servants to help, everything to make a fine feast. It must have made her very proud; she knew that when the feasting was over, the good pasha would visit her home and pay the respects and compliments of the guests to the best cook between Beirut and Damascus.

The pasha showed his gratitude in other ways. He gave Kbashy and her family the best house on his acres to live in. And he gave them a plot of ground to till rent-free. No one was supposed to know this, but when the pasha's servants made the annual rent collections, they always passed over my grandmother's crops.

As a result she was able to set aside a little nest egg. She knew what she wanted to do with it. Over in the prosperous little village of Ain Arab, with its busy water mills and fruitful vineyards, were several abandoned estates like the one she lived on. The owners had gone to America and left them in the care of relatives or tenants. They had been poorly tended or left to go back to weeds and thistles.

Someday she was going to buy one of them; the price would be cheap. The family would go there to live, she and my grandfather and their three sons. They would build it up and have tenants and make rent collections and acquire an independent life and security for their sons and for their old age. That was her dream. It was a beautiful dream for her, but it was destined to fail.

When her sons were grown they heard fabulous stories of a rich, fair land across the sea. "In America," they were told, "wheat grows like weeds." So one by one they sailed away, using Kbashy's nest egg to help buy their passage.

She was soon reconciled to the disappointment of her dream, but the loss of her sons was almost more than she could bear. "They are as good as dead," she would say, and she mourned them as if they had gone to their graves.

Then, after some years, I was born and the old dream came alive in another form. My mother had died giving me birth. Everybody expected me to die, too. But my grandmother, who lived twelve miles away, came donkey-back to Ain Arab to claim me for herself. "He shall not die," she said. "He shall live and I shall be his mother. His name shall be Salom, 'the Rescued One.' Nothing shall harm him, and nothing shall take him away. When I am old and feeble, he shall be the light and strength of my last days."

But now Kbashy had a problem. How was she to feed me, a motherless babe? In the backward parts of Syria life is almost as primitive as in Biblical times. There are no nurses, no doctors, no hospitals; there are no drugstores to sell nursing bottles; no grocery stores with shelves of condensed milk. And the milk of animals was not considered safe for a baby.

My grandmother solved the problem by begging milk of other mothers, and it did not matter much who the mother was. That's where the trouble came in. My grandmother did not discriminate between Christian, Mohammedan, Jewish, or Druse mothers. They all fed me. As a result I became the object of a strange fear and superstition. In Syria there is a saying that he who drinks the milk of a cow becomes like a cow. I had drunk the milk of Christians, so I should become a Christian. But I had also drunk the milk of Mohammedans. Would that make me a Mohammedan? No. I could not be a Christian and a Mohammedan at the same time. What was I, then? I was a child of Shaitan, the devil. Who else but the devil could inspire a baby to drink the milk of mortal enemies, of people of whom God disapproved? I was terrible. I would turn out to be a monster. I must be avoided. As a little boy I can remember distinctly certain mothers loudly scolding their children for playing with me; I remember one boy being beaten because he went out to the fields with me.

When I was about seven years old my grandmother was badly hurt in a fall from a donkey. The village goatkeeper set the broken limbs, and the men built a bed by laying a threshing board over a pair of sawhorses.

She was very sick for a long time after the fall. People came and went quietly and talked in whispers and shook their heads sadly, and some of them knelt and prayed. For days it seemed she was out of her head, talking in such a queer way and screaming so hard I was afraid to be near her. But after a while she felt better, and then she wanted me by her side all the time. "You won't leave me, my little candle," she would say. "I have so great need of thee now. I know now that God has sent you to me to be the light and strength of my last days."

Every morning when the weather allowed, some of the men carried Kbashy outdoors into the shade of a big old walnut tree. My job was to keep watch over her, to tend to her needs during the day. But really I hardly ever noticed that I was doing anything for her; she made everything so easy for me. It was those stories of hers.

"Tell me a story, Grandmother," I would say. "Tell me the story of the bad boy and the copper coins."

And then she would tell it, perhaps for the dozenth time, but with such freshness that I listened as enthralled as the first time she told it. And I shall never forget the first time she told the story of the bad boy and the copper coins, for she meant to teach me a lesson with it—a lesson she wanted me never to forget.

It was not long before her fall, and I had just had a fight. There was blood on my face from a cut on my forehead, and then red spots began to show up on my soiled robe. Frightened, I ran home to Kbashy, bawling at the top of my lungs and expecting the usual sympathy. She took one look at me, one look into the short street where we had been playing, and then leaped through the open door and lit out across the court in front of our house.

Four boys, yelling wildly and hurling stones and curses, were chasing my assailant toward his home at the other end of the village, and now my grandmother was in hot pursuit. They dodged in and out among earthen bake ovens, wooden plows, manure piles, and tethered donkeys and finally disappeared in a flurry of chickens around the corner of a stone hut. Left alone, apparently to bleed to death, I broke out and wailed more loudly than ever.

In a little while my grandmother came back. She was all out of breath and had a funny twinkle in her eyes. "Big wounds, Salom," she said, "should be tended first."

"Big wounds?" I repeated. "Is it a big wound?" I was about to cry all over again.

"No, no, Salom, but little wounds sometimes make big wounds, and little quarrels can make bad wars." I did not understand, but I knew that it had something to do with our fight.

My grandmother brought water from the earthen jug

which sat in the corner by the fireplace, and washed the blood and dirt from my face. Grinding some limestone between two stones, she sprinkled the resulting powder on my wound and tied it all up with a bandage ripped from an old headcloth. When she had finished she sat down in front of me and said, "Salom, we are going to have a party tonight, and Ali is going to be the guest of honor."

Ali, guest of honor! I could hardly believe my ears. Why, Ali was the boy who had stoned me!

Some of us boys had been entertaining ourselves at *kaab*, a sort of dice game played with colored animal bones by the children in some of our smaller villages in Syria. I thought I had caught Ali cheating and made a fuss about it. He insisted that I was seeing things, but after a lot of noisy argument the rest of us all agreed that the thing to do was to kick him out of the game. So we kicked him out, and he got good and mad and called me an insulting name. I came right back at him; *khanzir*, I called him—that is, a pig. And then he really blew up. I was a Christian; he was a Mohammedan. To call a pork-hating Mohammedan a pig is to court certain disaster; it's a real fighting word if there ever was one. Ali picked up a sharp stone and hurled it in my direction, with the results already described.

Now we were going to honor Ali with a party! I couldn't understand it; it didn't make sense.

But the party was held. Ali and his mother came, and

the other four boys and their mothers; we all had a very good time playing *kaab* and feasting heartily on nuts and raisins and dried figs, delicacies usually served only on holidays or to very special guests.

When the party was nearly over we all went outdoors and sat down under the stars on goat-hair mats. Ali sat beside me as if nothing had ever happened. We put our arms around each other, grinned again about the big head-cloth that bound up such a little wound, and tickled each other in the ribs.

After we were all seated in the circle, my grandmother made us quiet by clearing her throat and looking intently at each dark, moonlit face, as if to say, This is for you, and you, and you. "Once upon a time," she began, "there was a very bad boy. So bad he was that he would not hesitate even to tease and torment the most helpless people. One day he was playing in the street with a gang of rough boys, when an old man came hobbling along on a cane. When the bad boy saw him he said to his companions, 'Aha, watch me and you will see some fun.' Then he ran up behind the old man and kicked him in the seat so hard he sent him sprawling helplessly into the dust and sharp stones of the road.

"As the old man struggled to his feet, the bad boy and his friends laughed and gloated—from a safe distance, for besides being bad, they were afraid.

"When the old man got to his feet, he did a strange thing. He reached into his pocket and drew out three copper coins and called to the bad boy, 'Come here, my son,' he said, 'I have something for you.'

"But the boy was wary and would not come.

" 'Come, come, my boy, I have a present for you.'

"Still the boy did not come.

"So the old man threw a copper on the road, and the boy came and picked it up. Then the old man said, 'I want to compliment you on the extraordinary strength of your kick. No donkey in the land has the strength to kick so hard, and no donkey has such a good aim. It is indeed a most wonderful kick.'

"Then, offering the bad boy the other coppers, the old man said, 'Take these too, my son, and be glad. I only wish it were more. But I pray Allah that you will get a gold piece from the very next man who has the pleasure of your most wonderful and most powerful kick.'

"The boy thought this was a great stroke of fortune. He could hardly wait for another man to kick. But he was determined now to kick only one who was able to reward him amply with gold pieces.

"The very next day the bad boy was loafing at the village spring when a very rich-looking man rode up on a beautiful horse. The day was hot and the man was thirsty. Getting down from his horse, he leaned over the spring to drink of its cool, sparkling water.

" 'This is my golden chance,' thought the bad boy, and promptly he kicked the rich man so hard he upset him into the watering trough. But this time the bad boy did not run away. He stood by and laughed most loudly and waited greedily for the shower of gold to fall.

"Very strangely, the rich man did not think kindly of the kick. Instead of reaching into his pockets for gold, he seized a whip from his horse and threshed the boy until he cried for mercy. Then he leaped to his horse and rode off, leaving the bad boy to ponder the lesson which the poor old man with the cane intended for him to learn in the first place."

"Who is the bad boy?" I asked as soon as my grandmother had finished; of course, I was thinking of Ali.

"You were both bad boys," she said, "and the party, you see, is your copper coin."

"And the party is our copper coin," Ali repeated, his eyes brightening with the wonder of discovery.

"And the next time we get no gold coins?" said I.

"Next time we get whips," said Ali.

My grandmother winked a fat wink and nodded confirmation.

To hear the story of the bad boy and the copper coin was to remember all that. And there were many, many stories like that, mingled with our daily fare like the salt in our food—stories from the Bible, stories from the *Arabian Nights*, and stories, I am sure, that had no other source than my grandmother's imagination.

Just how much the world of my boyhood was a creation of her imagination, I shall never know. I do know that there was a time when there was no line between the things that are real and the things that are not; a time when they all ran together and were one world; when all things were true and all things were good and all things were beautiful.

I know that, almost every day of the three years she was confined to the threshing-board bed, there were hours when I was not in Ybose or Ain Arab or anywhere else you could reach by foot or by donkey. Yet those places to which I was transported were real to me, and the people who inhabited them were real, and the miraculous things they did were true and delightful.

The world was beautiful then, and so were the mountain above us and the valley around us—and so was the house we lived in. Besides all the people, the giants and dwarfs and fairies and jinn my grandmother made so real to me, there were the animals in the other room of our house. After a story at night it was fine to go to sleep with the lullaby of the stable in my ears. I should tell you about that, for few people realize what a wonderful institution is a stable.

The transactions which took place between the stable

and our living quarters involved not only meat and milk and eggs but a number of less tangible things—various disturbances, noises, smells which provided a subdued accompaniment to our lives. Sometimes, of course, it was not so subdued. For example, we had a lusty female donkey who, at certain predictable intervals, got her days and nights mixed and indelicately insisted upon broadcasting to the whole village, in the most unmusical voice possible, the amorous state of her impulses. But at night most of the stable noises were an indescribably sweet prelude to the warm drowsiness before sleep. You could feel them, warm and friendly, in your ears—the faint, familiar stir of animals, the soft whimpering of the hens, the occasional complaining of a disturbed rooster, the muffled bleat of a contented goat, the gentle tinkling from the bellwether scratching his fleas. There was something so intimate, so solid and comforting about those sounds; they gave you something to take hold of when you sank into the dark, mysterious caves of sleep.

When you woke up in the morning the stable was the first thing you heard. With the dawn a rooster somewhere in the village stretched his neck and shattered the village quiet with a crowing as shrill as a factory whistle. Then the competition set in. There was crowing first from one house and then from another and finally from all of them at once, like an orchestra tuning up. With brays and blats and bleats and whinnies thrown in, the din was enough to stir the sleepiest fellah from his most pleasant dreams. So everybody got up, and shortly, as if by prearrangement, the crowing tapered off and died out.

Yes, that was the beautiful world then, the big mountain and the sleepy little valley, the stable in the house, the games we children played, the stories my grandmother told —everything was just right.

But one day that world blew up in my face like a toy balloon. I awoke one morning with the last crowings of the roosters and went to my grandmother's bed. Almost always she was awake before I was. But this time she was not. I waited and waited, and when she did not wake up, I spoke to her. When I could not waken her, I ran to the fields and called two men. They said, "She is dead."

"Dead?" I said.

"Yes, her soul is gone."

"Her soul is gone. Where has it gone?"

"Her soul has gone to heaven."

"I want to go, too," I said.

"You cannot go. Your time is not yet."

They buried her in the burying place just below the pasha's house. Since Ybose had no priest, there was no service, no singing, no praying. She who had sung the chants at wakes and weddings for many had no chant to mourn the passing of her spirit. I wept long on her grave and then went away. I was a homeless waif, cast upon the mercy of the earth, but in no spirit to receive mercy, or take charity from any hand, for my grandmother had taught me it was sinful for an able-bodied boy to be a burden to anyone.

CHAPTER II

Gontoosy Sees It Through

HALFWAY BETWEEN BEIRUT AND DAMASCUS a narrow donkey trail leaves the main road and winds its way for about twelve miles through the rough, gray hills to the little Syrian village of Ain Arab—literally, Arab's Spring. Here, in this ancient, sleepy village, I was born and baptized in the Christian faith. Here it was that my grandmother came to claim me when my mother died. And to this town I now turned my uncertain footsteps in the hope of finding refuge. I was not sure that I ought to go, because things were getting bad and my people in Ain Arab already had too many mouths to feed. But since I knew nowhere else to turn, I went there.

On the way I came upon a battlefield strewn with the corpses of fallen soldiers—mangled and twisted bodies, stripped and looted of boots and belts and decaying like so many animals in the hot Syrian sun. For this was the

First World War, and armies were fighting across Syria, driving the people from their homes and laying many of the villages in ruins. I shall never forget the awfulness, the gripping horror, of that sight as long as I live. I was tired, hungry, and footsore, but the stench of rotting human flesh and the terrorizing sight of torn and blood-caked bodies changed my hunger into sickening repulsion, my fatigue into wide-eyed fear, and my bleeding feet into numb, unfeeling leather. Pursued by the thousand phantoms of those unburied bodies, I fled over sharp rocks, thorns, and thistles without feeling any pain.

As I drew near to Ain Arab, my footsteps faltered. Other fears came to replace the ones I had fled. There was only one home I could go to—my maternal grandmother's—and she was a struggling widow. I knew I would only be an added burden to her, just another hungry mouth to feed. I could not make myself feel I would be welcome. On that day the world seemed too small and crowded. From the distance I could see my grandmother's home with its high-arched door and whitewashed walls, the tall birch tree overshadowing it, and the small cluster of trees out front. That was the house I was born in, but could I now dare to hope for shelter in it? I didn't think so. My feet shuffled aimlessly, halfheartedly, on the dusty trail. Darkness was settling on the flat-roofed stone houses of Ain Arab when I arrived; from a few, faint flickers of light shone tiredly through the unglassed windows; the others were huddled dark masses against the hills.

On the edge of the village I met two girls I knew driving a donkey on the trail. One of them asked, "Have you come to say good-by?"

What was this! Come to say good-by? I could not understand.

"Didn't you know your grandmother is going away?"

"No."

"Yes, she is going on a long, dangerous journey—with your uncle Gibran. It is very exciting. We are going to have a big celebration tonight."

"Where are they going?"

"To Houran, to Jebel el Druse—to get grain. It is a long journey, and everybody is afraid for them because the road is very unsafe now."

Just then the girls remembered their donkey, which had gotten ahead of them, and they ran on, leaving me to ponder the implications of this unexpected turn of events.

I did not know what to do now, so I loitered on the edge of the village, keeping out of everybody's way.

After a while voices drifted to me from my grandmother's house. It was dimly lit with a few homemade tallow candles, and the shadows of people were gathering there—nearly the whole village, it seemed. I crept up as close as I could without being seen and listened to stray bits of conversation. It sounded more like a funeral than a farewell. Some of the women were weeping, and one old man's voice rose plaintively in pleading: "O Gontoosy, hear me, and do not go on this dangerous way. Better it is to stay, to starve and die here among friends, than to trust your life to thieves and the wolves of the wilderness. Who knows what sort of death or terrible fate will meet you in those mountains? Please, Gontoosy, think again and listen to us. Stay! *Stay!* STAY!"

My grandmother Gontoosy made reply: "You know well that I go not for my sake only, but for the sake of the soul of Asaad. He died leaving these many debts unpaid, owing you money which you loaned him to carry on his trading. With that money he bought this grain in Houran which is not delivered. I go only to collect that we may have what is ours and you may have what is yours. God willing, I shall return safely. You shall all be paid to the very last grain. Our children—my children and your children—shall not go hungry, and God knows, they will go hungry if we do not get food from the outside."

After that I knew I could never throw myself on my grandmother's charity. She had enough, and more than enough, without me. I sat there in the dark, huddled sadly on a hard stone, until the last of the guests went home.

Where now could a cold, hungry, sleepy orphan find refuge? I thought of going to the valley just outside the village to hunt out a small cave, but I was afraid of the wolves and hyenas. Then I realized that I was not far from the village bake oven. To that I repaired at once, poking inquisitively into it with a stick to see if any stray dogs or rats had gotten there first. Finding none, I went in. It was just like the one in Ybose. Scores of times I had stood by my grandmother Kbashy's side and watched her skillfully manipulate a round ball of dough with her forearms, stretching it thinner and thinner into a sheet of bread hardly thicker than a piece of newspaper and just as big. I had seen her slap it deftly on the sizzling hot cylinder for baking, then peel it off when it was done, and repeat the action until there was a stack of bread big enough to last us a couple of weeks. How my mouth watered for some of that bread now, for I hadn't eaten for two days!

There were still a few live embers in the cylinder, and these leaped into flame when stirred and fed with a handful of dry sticks. After taking off my robe and shaking it over the flames until the lice rolled off, I put it back on, curled up in a corner, and slept until the roosters started crowing.

With the morning I quickly got up and slipped out of the village. I didn't want my aunts who were to keep things going in my grandmother's absence to see me here, and besides I wanted to find a high place where I could lie hidden and watch my grandmother's departure. Later that morning I saw her and Uncle Gibran riding up the trail on two donkeys loaded with feed sacks. She took the road that leads to Houran while my aunts and other relatives wept and waved good-by and said God's blessing on them. My own tears they never saw, and my own wordless blessings they never heard.

While the people in Ain Arab went about their accustomed chores and tasks, I began an unwonted and difficult search for something to still the gnawing hunger in my stomach. First, though, I knelt in the grass and said the prayer Kbashy had taught me to say before partaking of the earth's bounty which God had made. All around me were the gray hills and the pink hills and the stunted trees and the crawling vines. Spring was on the land, and young leaves and flowers were growing, but there was little that I could eat. I spied a bird's nest in the branches of a tree overhead. I climbed up and found several eggs. I was so hungry that I ate them raw. Other trees I climbed and other nests I robbed, until my emptiness felt not quite so empty. Roots, too, there were that twisted my mouth with their bitterness, but they were better than nothing.

Foraging thus for food, I came pretty soon over a hill; below in the public pasture were the cows and goats of the village. There, lying in the shade of a tree, was the goatherd. I lay down behind a rock and peeked over the hill, watching the grazing flocks and wishing I might have a

great long drink of delicious goat's milk. For a long time I
lay, wishing more and more for that drink as the sun grew
hotter and hotter, and then I saw a goat, several goats,
grazing near a break in the opposite ridge. The goatkeeper
appeared to be asleep. Anyway, it was worth the chance.
I dashed around to the other side and, when the opportunity was ripe, struck quickly. I had my goat, but she was
dragging me over the rough ground, skinning my knees
and elbows and tearing my already tattered robe. But I
hung on and she stopped, and I milked her into my little
hand-knit cap, which was so dirty and greasy that it actually
stood up. I did not know anything about microbes then,
and I don't think they knew anything about me. We just
ignored each other.

The milk was so good, I went back every day and risked
my hide for it. Then the goatherd caught me in the very act
of milking.

He raised his staff as if to beat my head, but I threw out
my arm and cried out, "Please, please, Yousef Effendi,
don't beat me. I am only hungry and I mean no harm."

Slowly he lowered his staff, his eyes still glowering.

"If I didn't know you and your people, I would kill you.
But why do you do this? You can't be so poor that you have
to go hungry and steal. Your grandmother, your aunts,
surely they could feed you. Or are you doing this for
mischief?"

their skinny little donkeys loaded with pathetic little bundles of hurriedly rescued articles, many of them useless in their fight for survival in the wilderness. Most of them came bearing the remains of their earthly possessions on their backs. Fine, home-loving people they were—rugged peasants, tradesmen, professional people—and now they were reduced in a single stroke to the degradation and misery of hapless beggars, frightened fugitives of the Syrian wastelands.

They told such wild tales we could hardly believe them. They told how their children had been murdered in cold blood before their very eyes, and their fathers and mothers, too, who were too old to flee. They told of whole villages evacuated, looted, burned and destroyed. They told of people being set out on the march with no place to go, toddling children and wailing old people. They told how their homes had been commandeered to serve as barracks for drunken soldiers and even as stables for their horses and donkeys, and how the beasts behaved far more decently than their masters. They told how whole plantations of precious mulberry trees, indispensable to their silkworm industry, had been cut down for fuel. They told of a salt shortage so severe that the women walked long, weary miles to the sea with jugs on their heads to get sea water, only to have the soldiers make a brutal sport out of shooting the vessels from their heads. They told of gallant patriots, brave men of the gardens and vineyards of the Lebanon who spoke up for freedom, decency, and humanity, being strung up to their own trees which they had planted and reared and loved.

There were many wild, incredible tales like that—and tales of courage and heroism, of narrow escapes, of super-human deeds and superhuman endurance—but we didn't doubt them long, for soon we too came to experience the same hardships and horrors and see the same display of fortitude and noble humanity.

Yes, before that summer was over, we were all praying for the safe return of Gontoosy and Gibran, for they stood between us and a menacing scarcity, perhaps even slow death by starvation, especially if things kept getting worse the way they had been. But would they come back? Or had they already been set on by wolves, or thieves, or hungry soldiers? All we could do in the village was to pray and wait.

In the meantime we were visited by two kinds of plagues: one of locusts, the other of men, and of the two the latter was the worse. The locusts came in summer; our priest used to chant, "All good things come from above," but this was an evil thing that now befell us from the heavens.

The vines in the vineyards were splendid green, and the wheat was just getting gold from the sun. And then they came—by the billions—and they darkened the skies and filled the air with a great whirring of wings. It really frightened me. They fell on everything, the fields and fig trees, the vineyards and the pastures, until every inch of earth was crawling black with them, and yet the sky was full of them. They devoured everything they touched, the bark of trees, the feathers of chickens, and the hair of goats. We went out to fight them with brooms and poles and shouting of voices and with rattling of stones in tins. We cried, "The sea gulls are coming, the sea gulls are coming," but either they did not understand Arabic or they thought we were fooling; which we were.

And on they came, always more of them, in clouds and clouds, hiding the sun from sight, and hiding the earth with their wings. They ate and spawned and died by the millions until the fields and vineyards were covered with their corpses and eggs and the creeping new generation.

After they were gone there were sadness and foreboding in the valley, and the sadness was for what the locusts had done and the foreboding was for what the tax collectors would do.

They came, the tax collectors did, in the time of harvest. They stayed in our houses as if they owned them. They watched every move we made lest we steal our own wheat from under their noses. When the wheat was piled by our houses—in small piles outdoors, for there was not much because of the locusts—they placed the great seal of the Turkish government on the wheat and went to bed—on our mats. If the seal was broken in the morning, it was the owner who suffered. So every owner and the members of his family lived in fear of the seal being broken. They stayed up all night and took turns guarding the wheat piles against thieves and stray dogs and cats and anything else that might break the soft seal on the wheat. Those were the days when even the wind was feared because it could blow up strong and break the great seal, too; but since you cannot catch the wind to punish it, you simply catch the owner and punish him.

Finally the levy of wheat was taken, and the levy of all the other crops; the officials went away, leaving us to struggle along with what remained until the spring.

Still Gontoosy and Uncle Gibran did not come.

And yet the tax gatherers did not fail to come, again and again, raiding the village systematically, house by house, room by room, person by person. Nothing was too small or insignificant or useless-looking for them to seize. Every scrap of metal, even down to the tiny iron points on the wooden plows, was carted off to feed the insatiable war machine. When they started to empty the feathers out of our pillows to make sandbags, my aunt Zarefy was ready to fight. But there was really nothing one could do—that is, by fighting.

But the people of Ain Arab had their own ways of resisting these seizures, and sometimes it took a lot of nerve. One time, I remember, we spirited away almost the entire collection from my grandmother's house under the very nose of a Turkish officer. He was looting the house, going in and out, dumping the things he wanted in the doorway. Every time he went in for more spoil, we grabbed up the collected plunder and hid it behind rocks in a near-by gully. He thought his soldiers were taking it.

Not only did the people try to defeat the tax collections. The men also resisted military service. Not that they were cowards. They would gladly have fought for a cause they believed in. But they did not believe in the cause of being oppressed by the Turks or by anyone else. So some of the men mutilated themselves—cut off their fingers, broke their arms, or poured scalding water on their feet. Others hid out in the hills, asking the people in the villages to lie about their whereabouts when the Turkish officers inquired about them.

One day a group of conscription officers of the government came to Ain Arab. They had been there before and had gone away without getting so much as a smell of a soldier. This time they rode directly to the spring where five or six of us children were playing. They were very nice to us, but we had been warned about that. They gave us money and sweets to eat, and we took them. They invited us to hold their horses while they drank, and we held them. They boosted us into the beautiful saddles and rode us up and down the trail.

Then they asked us where Saleem Khoury was.

"He went to Palestine," we said.

"Where is Najeeb Sumra?"

"He is dead. The funeral was last month."

"Where is Yousef Abdo?" they asked.

"He was kicked by a donkey, and he died, too," we replied.

"Where is Iskander Habib?"

"We don't know. We haven't seen him for a long time," we said.

Apparently satisfied, the officers got on their horses and started to ride off, when they came upon a boy grazing a calf on a hillside near the village. They stopped and asked him where all the men were. He told them. As the officers rode off to round up their victims, the boy remembered something and shouted to them to come back. "I forgot to tell you about Ibrihim Shamas. He is down by the water mill." That was his own uncle, the most sought of all the men, a strong man, a good soldier.

Nobody really blamed the boy. He was only trying to be obliging. Besides, someone had forgotten to tell him to lie. Nevertheless there was much sadness and gnashing of teeth in the village that day.

Those were the terrible days. You hardly remembered things having been any better. You had never heard of better lands where children grew up in peace and plenty, comfort and security. You were just a child seeing and feeling brutality, living in fear and trembling, taking for granted that things were like this all the time in all places. You forgot that you had once been a smaller child in a quiet little village. You forgot the sweetness and beauty of the days your grandmother told such wonderful stories. You remembered only the living nightmare of present misery and dread.

Dreadful things happened that stamped themselves on you forever; years later they come back to you so vividly it seems they are happening again. Once, for example, a lone Turkish soldier came to Ain Arab and proceeded to ransack the homes, piling goods in the street for the tax collector's donkey caravan to pick up later. In one home, I don't know what it was that irritated him, but he raised his boot and kicked a crippled child lying on a mat on the floor and sent it hurtling across the room. At the same instant the horrified mother screamed her anguish. Then a dead, sickening silence. Then such a mother's sobbing as would tear your heart out.

Those are the things you never forget. When you start writing your story, you have to go around and ask a lot of the older people about how things happened when you were a child, because you remember them only vaguely, and some you do not remember at all. But some things are stamped on your memory forever, and something in you remembers them even when you try to forget them. You wake up in the dead of night, and the terror of it is upon your mind and upon your body, and you cannot throw it off, the weight of it is so heavy. There is some evil spirit, some demon of those events that haunts you all your life. No matter how grotesque and distorted the demon becomes from its original self, no matter what awful new shapes he takes, it is the same old demon of that event. In those dreadful days my demons were born, and some of them are with me yet. They were the demons of man's inhumanity to man, the demons of fearsome events, of brutal rape and plunder, of aching hunger and all manner of wretchedness.

With the cold coming on we went to the woodlands and ate the bitter acorn and gathered it for the winter. We dug in the hills for the wild onion, the wild greens, and the wild root of everything that could be eaten.

Then at last came the day of great rejoicing. My grandmother and Uncle Gibran were sighted in the distance, riding on their little gray donkeys, followed from afar by a caravan of camels escorted by Arabs from Houran. Almost half the village ran down the trail to greet them. Gontoosy we greeted with great shouts of joy, and smothered her feet in kisses. She was hailed as a Joseph bringing salvation to a starving village.

Having arrived in the courtyard of Gontoosy's home, the Arabs shouted, "Ick, Ick," and the great clumsy camels knelt to be relieved of their loads, for they were very heavy.

The town crier went to the top of the house and shouted the joyous news: "On this day, Mrs. Asaad Gibran, widow of the late Asaad Gibran—may God rest his soul in peace—will pay, in the harvested wheat of Houran, all the honest debts of her husband. Come now and receive your just due."

Most of the wheat was cached in secret places in the hills—along with many other things, and guns and ammunition—to keep it away from the tax gatherers.

And so a village lived a better winter than otherwise because an honest widow braved the perils of war and wilderness to keep faith with the spirit of her departed husband and with those who had trusted him.

Encouraged by the success of Gontoosy and Uncle Gibran, about ten men of Ain Arab determined to make the long journey to the fields of Houran to bring back wheat for their families. They never returned. It was guessed that they had been set upon by a roving band of Arabs and murdered.

CHAPTER III

Pigs Will Be Pigs

AT LAST THE GREAT WAR ENDED—but not the hunger of the people, nor the rapacious demands of the Turks, nor the prowling of the robber bands. The years after the war's end were hectic and chaotic. They were sad and hungry years. The Turks had been defeated, yes, and the news had at last come to our village, but we did not at first believe it. We had heard those rumors before, and they had always been false. So when the rumor came again that at last the fighting was over, we were skeptical and there was no rejoicing. There were plenty of petty officials and hangers-on who took advantage of our disbelief. Soldiers and officials still kept coming, seizing our donkeys and our wheat and keeping terror alive in our hearts. Some of them probably did not know that the war was ended. But others knew, and they tried to bluff us into believing otherwise, insisting that we were still subject to the Turkish government, which needed our produce to carry on the war.

As we became convinced of the end of hostilities and certain of the defeat of the Turks and Germans, we resisted. The people had a thousand scores to settle with the enemy who had insulted, humiliated, robbed, and murdered them for centuries. There were at least a hundred good rifles in Ain Arab. So our village was a hot hell for any Turk bold or dumb enough to show his head there. How the people hoped, waited, and prayed that a certain one, Abn Khaleel, the one who had kicked the crippled child, would pay them a visit now! Luckily for him, he never came.

The problem of getting enough to eat was still with us, and it was especially with me, a ragged, half-starved orphan, who was cast upon the mercy and charity of other people. It bothered me to feel that I was a burden; sometimes I thought I was not wanted. One day the chance came to remedy this. I was loafing at the spring on the outskirts of Ain Arab when a farmer from the neighboring village of Kfer Kuk stopped there to water his donkey. The beast had a very heavy load of two big boxes and was all out of breath from struggling up the long, steep slope. While the animal was drinking at the stone trough I heard the oddest noises, squealings, and mutterings coming from the boxes.

"Seman Khamees," I said, "what is it you have in those boxes?"

"Pigs," he said.

"Pigs?" I cried. "Pigs, real pigs, live ones? Please, could I see them?"

"Certainly," he said, reaching his hand into a box and bringing one out. It squirmed and squealed and grunted. Just a little bit of a fellow he was, no bigger than a cat, with a queer, blunt snout. So that is what a Moslem is when you are mad at him—a pig! I reached out to touch him and then pulled my hand back quickly.

"Don't be afraid," said Khamees. "He won't bite."

"What are you going to do with them?" I asked.

"Raise them. They make wonderful meat, better even than mutton."

"How big do they get?"

"Oh, they grow very big, get to weigh hundreds of pounds."

"I wish I could see them when they are grown," I said. And then Khamees made the most astonishing offer. "Go with me to my home in Kfer Kuk and I will give you the job of raising and herding them. You can live with me in my house, and I will buy you clothes and even a pair of shoes. You would like to have a pair of shoes, wouldn't you?"

I would. I had not had a pair of shoes since Kbashy died.

Since then I had picked thorns and thistles out of my bare feet, and walked on hot stony soil until my face was almost set in a perpetual grimace.

So I became a swineherd. Have you ever herded pigs? If you haven't, don't ever do it! Pigs don't herd. They have no social instinct, no desire for any kind of fellowship, no urge to organize or go around together in parties. Cattle will graze together. Horses will nuzzle affectionately, nose to rump. Sheep will love a shepherd and heed his call. Goats will follow a leader, and they have an instinct for leadership. But pigs! There is no way known to God or man by which they can be herded, regimented, or driven in a straight line to any definite goal. They have only one love in life—dirt! They live in it, love it, roll in it, sleep in it, and eat it. If they cannot find dirt, they will manage to make some. Their one goal in life is dirt, and since you can find dirt anywhere, a pig will go anywhere—and he does. The only way you can manage pigs is with a fence; and we had no fence.

But I didn't know the nature of this new animal yet; neither did Khamees. My only feeling then was one of innocent, uneducated joy at being able to earn my own living by taking care of these cute little beasts with the long, funny snouts and the soft, throaty noises.

My troubles began the very first day. It was plain from

the start that the pigs did not want to go where we wanted them to go. Khamees said that was because they were young and needed a little training. So he and his family helped me to drive them to the mountain pasture about two miles away, where the sheep, goats, and cattle were accustomed to graze during part of the year. For my new task I was provided with a shepherd's staff, two animal skins for my lunch and water, and a variety of goat calls with which to keep my charges under control. After a good deal of running and chasing and coaxing and calling, we managed to establish the flock where it belonged. "They herd just like goats," Khamees told me as he left me alone with my flock. "All you have to do is to keep them together. Use your voice and you won't have to use your legs so much."

Almost at once the herd disintegrated. There were something like fifteen pigs. No two of them were attracted by the same object or moved by the same impulse. Each one went off by himself to find what he could find. Instead of eating the leaves, grasses, and weeds, as it was intended they should do, they proceeded to uproot the earth with their long, rugged noses and to eat the loosened dirt. Before I could make any plans for them they had disappeared into the rocks, bushes, and tall timber in and around the pasture. Remembering Khamees' advice to use my voice to keep them together, I began to shout goat calls. It didn't work.

So I hunted them out and ran them back to the central place. But by the time I returned with one, the others had disappeared. All day long I panted, cried, and chased after those rodents, up and down the hills, over and around the rocks and trees. The harder I tried to tame and train those pigs, the wilder and more ignorant they became. I tried creeping up on them softly in the hope of catching one and proving my kindness, but just when I got close enough to grab one, he snorted and ran off. My patience gave out and I threw stones at them, angrily delighted when I hit one. Then, with stifled sobs aching in my throat, I ran after some more of them. Tired out, I tried the goat calls again. Then I stalked them with new determination, but always they eluded me, and always they were scattered as widely as it is possible for fifteen animals to be scattered without leaving the country. I sat down and cried. I called all the familiar goat calls and prayed God to help me. I ran and chased pigs some more until I thought my lungs would burst. I sat down and cried again. I wailed at the top of my lungs and called upon all creation to witness the terrible agony of my helplessness. I cursed the day I was born—and the day the pigs were born. But nothing worked. The best I could do was to keep them from leaving the country. And some of them, I thought, must already have done so.

Night came. The pigs were gone. I could not return to Kfer Kuk without them. Somewhere out here in the darkness they were. I stumbled around, angry and crying, filling the air with anguish and the earth with tears, stumbled in the rocks and bushes and trees, once in a while scaring up a pig. Immediately he scampered out and hid in a new place. If I found two or three of them together, it was either by accident or because they couldn't see each other in the dark to keep out of each other's company.

I sat down on a rock and devoted myself to hating pigs. Now I did not blame the Mohammedans. They were right. They had the right religion! I would gladly have embraced any faith which made the fervent hating of pigs the first and bounden religious duty.

When Khamees finally found me, he had ten or a dozen men with him. He was very angry. "At least you could try to keep them in Syria," he cried. "Don't you know if you let those pigs get over into Turkey the Moslem government will shoot them?"

It was nearly dawn when we got back to the village with the pigs.

The next day we were all too tired to take the pigs to pasture, but the following day Khamees said he was going to teach them to behave like decent goats or kill every one of them. He put five decent goats out in front to lead them, and he and I got behind to prevent retreat. It was useless. The pigs would not be led and they would not be driven. We could not even get them started out of the village. So

Khamees, a mean look in his eye, went after his horse. I felt sorry for the pigs, but it was very funny to see a big man on a great horse chase a little fifteen-pound pig all over Kfer Kuk. Even the Druses, who hated these animals and called them rats, had a hilarious time, going into fits of laughter every time a pig broke from the herd. Khamees got mad and said it was the Druses who were the rats and that he could whip any two of them with one hand tied behind his back. The Druses said it served him right to be tormented like this by pigs—and it served the pigs right, too.

Much as I shared the Mohammedan contempt for pigs, I began to be afraid that they were going to cause trouble in the village—and they did.

For several months I had been tending my unruly charges. Their deportment had by no means improved. In fact it had gotten much worse. I lost and found them dozens of times a day. Instead of gaining hundreds of pounds, as Khamees had been told they would, they became skinnier and skinnier. No matter how hard I tried to run them around to where the eating was better, they became gaunter, bonier, and uglier. I think they were a big disappointment to my boss. He took to blaming me for their bad behavior and runty appearance, and he took to beating me when they got out of control. As for me, I would have welcomed almost any catastrophe—fire, earthquake, war—anything which would relieve me of this grievous relationship.

At last the catastrophe came, but not the one I had prayed for. It had rained hard almost all of one day. The clay underfoot was soft and heavy, charged with sharp stones and thorns which bit into my bare feet like so many swine's teeth. Driving my exasperating herd home that night, I could not keep up with it. Time and again I had to stop to pick thorns from my feet and remove lumps of mud from between my toes. On the edge of the village my unchaperoned charges scattered to the four winds. Some of them strayed into a garden owned by a Druse peasant. I came up just as one of the servants was chasing the despised beasts from the field. He was tearing up as much garden as they were.

When he spied me, sliding down the muddy hill into the village, he cried, "You unholy Christian dog! You let these filthy, infidel swine desecrate my master's garden. Do you not know he will kill me if he finds these unholy pigs ruining his crops?"

I started to answer, but before I could do so my head and shoulders were smothered in a rain of blows. Crack! Whack! Thump! Thump! CRASH! When I came to, the Druse servant was gone. So were the pigs. My face was bleeding and throbbing with pain. My legs and shoulders smarted and ached. I walked and stumbled into the village to Khamees' house.

When Khamees heard my story, he was enraged. "Swine, dogs, devils!" he cried. "Those unholy beasts never learn a lesson. But they shall learn now. I'll make them pay for this. They'll never beat a Christian again."

He leaped across the room, seized his gun, and ran outside. Five shots he fired into the air. It was the Christian call to arms. In short order several score of men, all armed with rifles, were gathered in the *saha,* which is the center of the village. Khamees brought me out of the house and stood me in a circle of blazing eyes.

"Look at him. See what those infidels have done to a Christian. What they do to one of us they do to all of us. Ever since I bought those pigs to raise, they have been spoiling for trouble. They call my animals rats. They laugh at me when I drive them. They make coarse and unholy jokes about them. They sneer and taunt and jeer, and now they beat up my swineherd because a few pigs get into a Druse garden. I have held my tongue long enough. Too long. Now my patience is given out. These *khanzirs* must be taught a lesson they shall never forget."

Then, across the way, the Druses appeared. They had their rifles, too, but slung over their shoulders. They were walking toward us with their hands free. Every Christian defender lowered his rifle for firing. The Druses kept walking, step by step nearer, their feet beating out the steady, mounting rhythm of doom. My heart was pounding like

a galloping horse. Then they stopped. The leader slowly
lifted his hand in truce.

"For what cause do you spring to arms?" he asked. It was
the man who owned the garden, a wise and venerable old
sheik, with a white beard and a countenance like Moses'.

Khamees, without lowering his rifle, answered, "A
Christian has been beaten by a Druse, and when one of us
is beaten, we are all beaten; when one is insulted, all are
insulted. We demand retribution."

"Let us talk," said the old sheik.

So a conference was held. The Druses made apologies.
The servant was punished. The Christians were satisfied.
My head and back still ached.

But I breathed with deep and thankful relief. I told
Khamees that the old sheik was like Kbashy, a "father of
peace." He told me to hold my tongue. I said that if he had
gotten me a pair of shoes the way he promised, this would
never have happened. He cursed me and said the Druse
beating served me right.

So the next day I ran away. I did not want to see any
more religious trouble. Besides, I hated pigs—hated them
with a deep, passionate, ineradicable, Mohammedan hate.

CHAPTER IV

Passport to Heaven

I COULD THINK OF nowhere else to go, so now I retraced my steps to Ain Arab. It was Christmas time, and, the night before, a soft, wet blanket of snow had fallen. It lay thick over the hills as far as the eye could see. A warm winter sun was shining on the snow and made it sparkle so hard you had to squint your eyes tight against the glare. The trees were draped with snowy white furs and leaned toward one another as if to hoard among themselves the scant warmth from the sun. It was really beautiful. But I could not enjoy it. I was not happy, and when you are not happy the earth cannot be happy either.

Of course, I was glad to be away from Kfer Kuk, from that unpredictable volcano of hate which inspired the relations between the Druses and Christians, and from those unpredictable, exasperating pigs. Yet in my heart a black dejection was growing, and fear dragged at my heels like chains. Where could I go? Where did I belong? Where was my home? Who cared what happened to me?

How cruel and empty the world was then, how lonesome and forsaken; a place where hunger never ceased, and where the hunger of the belly was as nothing compared with the hunger of the heart; a place where you could expect fear to leap out of every new experience; a place where an indefinable restlessness and longing poked at your vitals like a stick ceaselessly stirring a fire.

My spirit would gladly have fled back to the days when Kbashy was alive; when there was a roof over my head and plenty of good cooked wheat, mutton, bread, and fruit to eat—and stories to fill you with a happy wonder. But those days were gone forever. I felt the loss keenly, especially at this Christmas time. If misfortune had any other blows for me, I was sure they would soon fall.

Yet such are the tides of fate, or whatever you want to call it, that now, without the slightest warning, I was to experience one of the most amazing moments of my life— yes, *the* most amazing moment, the turning point on which all my future life was to rest, about which it was to revolve as the wheel on the hub. My life was leading up to the hour of awakening and enchantment. I am not fooling. I am not exaggerating. I am telling you the truth. Not that I recognized the meaning of the approaching miracle. By no means. Not that it was going to be all unmitigated blessing. It was not. It was a very mixed thing. But from that moment my life was filled, and there was a groping toward a fulfillment which I had not known or even remotely felt before. And out of that hour were to flow the most exquisite pleasures and the sharpest pains, disappointments, frustrations, doubts, fears, and evil temptations—and new hopes, new thrills, new enchantments.

Just how it all came about is still something of a mystery to me. I cannot help but think—indeed, I have often thought —that a kind of Providence must have shaped the circumstances and guided the people, the deeds, and the words that brought me the great and beautiful revelation.

I hardly know how to begin to tell you about it, yet there is what seems to be a natural, inevitable movement and sequence that bore me on and up to the unexpected discovery. If you are to get anything of the feeling I had when the truth burst upon me, I think I should tell it, as nearly as I can, just the way it happened. And that isn't easy.

Back again in Ain Arab, I found work with an old widow whom everybody called Boomy, which means The Owl, because she had a high shrill voice and was always using it to shriek at her neighbors, with whom she managed to be at odds most of the time. My jobs were many and seasonal: bringing wood in from the timber; feeding and watering the animals; making cow dung into patties for fuel in winter; clearing the fields of stones, thorns, and weeds; keeping stray animals, foxes, and thieves out of the vineyard; picking figs, grapes, and mulberries and helping with the harvest of wheat and lentil. For all this I was to be paid one Turkish pound or its equivalent in wheat at the end of seven months. In addition I was to get my keep, plus shoes and clothing.

There is one man in Ain Arab to whom I am eternally indebted. Had it not been for his inspiring help and friendship I might never have stumbled into the destiny waiting for me. His name was George Nimur. He was a big man physically, thick as a barrel in the chest and strong as an ox. He was supposed to be stronger at lifting weights than any three—or maybe it was four—men in that town and the fiercest fighter in the region. It was told that he had once beaten his equally burly brother within an inch of his life, and people said if he would do that to his brother, what would he do to a stranger!

But I don't believe he did it. George Nimur was big, but he was gentle. He was quiet. He was not a quarrelsome man. And he was religious. Some people said he wasn't, but I know that wasn't true. He had a lot more religion than many people who make a big noise about it. I know, because he used to talk to me about God and the good life, and he made it so simple and down-to-earth that I was always reminded of the way Kbashy talked about those things.

There were some people afraid of George Nimur. I think it was because of the way he criticized the Church. He said, for example, too many priests read the Bible without understanding it or even wanting to understand it. " 'Blessed are the peacemakers,' " he once quoted from the Sermon on the Mount. "Do any of the priests know what that means? Do they know how much it involves? No. They think peace is easy, that you can talk your way to it. That is why the world never has peace. If you want peace you have to get to the bottom of things, and when you get to the bottom what do you find? Lies. Sometimes only a little lie, but even little lies can make big trouble. Why, I could start a war in this village with just one little lie. After that I could tell the truth all the time, and the more truth I told, the worse the fighting would get. All I have to do is to go to Ibrihim Zany and tell him that Aaron Shami said he was a thief and a liar. Now that would be a lie, because Aaron never said it. But it would be the only lie I would tell. Then Ibrihim would get mad and say that Aaron was a thousand times a thief and a liar. Then I would run to Aaron and tell him what Ibrihim had said about him, that he was a thousand times a thief and a liar. Since Ibrihim had actually said it, I would not now be lying. Well, it

would go back and forth like that, all the time getting
worse and worse. People would take sides till half the
village would be set against the other half. That is the way
a lot of trouble starts in this village and in every village.
It starts with one little lie, and then that little lie clings like
a bur to all the truth told after that, so that even all the
truth is a lie. But do the priests know that when they say,
'Blessed are the peacemakers'? No. They never get behind
the words. They do not know that behind the seeming
truth of both sides of every quarrel there is concealed a lie.
They read without knowing what they read."

The manner of my meeting this strong, wise man was
as follows. One day his son Tanos and I were sitting in the
shade of a stone hut and I was telling Tanos some of the
stories Kbashy used to tell me. We heard a noise behind us,
and when we looked up, there at the corner of the hut was
Tanos' father, smiling and nodding his head with pleased
approval. "May God bless your lips," he said to me. And
then to Tanos, "Listen to Salom, my son, listen to him
with all your heart. See how beautifully he speaks. He is
only a waif. He has no father or mother to encourage him.
He has never been in school a day. Yet he loves wisdom
like gold and speaks it like honey. He makes himself learn
and tells stories like a good teacher. If you would apply
yourself the way he does, you could do just as well. Isn't
that right, Salom?"

I nodded my head, not knowing what else to do.

From that time on, George Nimur took a special interest in me. We used to go off together and sit on the rocks or stumps or in the shade of an oak or mulberry tree, where he would listen encouragingly while I told some of the many Bible stories or *Arabian Nights* tales that I had heard from my grandmother. Then he would help me to understand them better, and I became as one of his sons to him.

One day he told me that he wanted me to go away to school, to a seminary, to study for the priesthood. He would pay my way when he could afford it. If I studied real hard, he said, I would become a good priest who would understand the Bible when he read it and who could help people to live the way Christ meant them to live. He told me about schools, teachers, books, the many wonderful things to be learned, till I was stirred to the depths with the thought of going to school. Those were happy hours and happy days. George Nimur was like a very father to me, and I felt like a son. Somewhere since I once read the definition that "education is encouragement." That is what George Nimur did for me. He wakened a hope in me, a dream, and he kept it alive so it could not be rubbed out.

Then, just when I was so filled with this blazing passion for going away to school to learn of all the marvelous things of the wide world, the school in Ain Arab was reopened. During the war it had been closed for want of a teacher, or for lack of money to pay a teacher. Also, in one of the raids on the village the school had been partly destroyed. For a long time it had stood open to the wind and blowing dirt, abandoned to the spiders and mice. Now some of the women cleaned up one of its four rooms. A few books were scared up and a teacher hired. His name was Elias Khoury, the son of the village priest.

In Ain Arab a teacher was idolized with the same love and reverence as a priest. That was because the two subjects diligently taught in the school, reading and writing, were the magic keys to the Bible—and to all truth and wisdom. Every parent coveted these abilities for his children as a sign of real distinction for the whole family. If at least one member of your home could not decipher a printed page or write a letter, you were in disgrace. And it was painful to receive a letter and have to confess that neither you nor anyone else in your family could read it.

So, when the school opened, how I longed to attend! But how could I? I was still working for the Boomy. And I did not have the fee—about twenty cents a month. Everybody was still very poor from the war, and I did not dare to ask my grandmother for help, or George Nimur either. With their large families I knew they had all they could do to send their own children. So I just went on working.

Sometimes, however, when work was slack, I would go to the school grounds to play with the other children during recess. This was a rare privilege, but what a dejection and disappointment was in my heart when the schoolmaster called a halt to the play and my companions filed back into the schoolroom, leaving me alone outside!

I must have looked as hungry and forlorn as I felt, because one day the schoolmaster asked me how I would like to go to school. The very thought so thrilled and overwhelmed me that I could only nod my head with bashful eagerness. He invited me in. Some of the pupils were sitting on benches; others sat cross-legged on the floor. Their eyes popped when they saw me. You couldn't really blame them. Here I was, a ragged little orphan with no clothes but a rag around my waist. The hot Syrian sun had scorched my skin to the color of earth, and my hair was long and hopelessly tangled like vines in a vineyard. I had no money, no parents, no social standing; nothing but suspicions of a dubious origin and talk of the devil; yet here I was going to school. It was amazing even in backward Syria.

Aside from several benches the only other piece of furniture in the schoolroom was a crude, wooden desk. The walls were rough stone chinked with clay and devoid of decoration. The floor was earthen, polished to a smooth hard shine by vigorous rubbing with smooth round stones. The whole thing would have been discouraging to any child used to the beauty and convenience of a modern school. But to me it was the next thing to heaven. I was almost thirteen years old then, and this was my first day in school—a day to be remembered forever, a day that filled me with happiness.

I sat down on the dirt floor, facing the teacher's desk. My first assignment was to learn the letters of the Syrian alphabet. I bent myself to this task with hungry enthusiasm. My eagerness must have greatly impressed the schoolmaster from the very first, because he took a special interest in my progress. He gave me a good deal of attention, sometimes talked to me during recess, and occasionally shared his scanty noon meal with me.

The days and months that followed were among the happiest I have ever known. Even Boomy shared my enthusiasm, and she often let me off so I could spend a day in school.

Elias Khoury was a very strict teacher. He had to be. He was expected to make the children mind not only in school but in the village as well. In this respect he was a sort of juvenile-delinquency officer. If boys got into mischief, raided somebody's vineyard, threw stones at the sheep, broke windows, swore in public or fell to fighting among themselves, part of the blame fell on the schoolmaster, and the responsibility of correction was his. For this purpose he kept a frequently stolen collection of sticks of graded sizes in the schoolroom, each stick suited to a certain degree of severity, since the punishment must fit the crime.

The parents generally stood squarely behind the school-master in all his enforcements. A mother would say to him in the presence of her guilty son, "You whip him till the flesh falls off, and send me the bones." Luckily for the culprit this was an extravagant command, but it was usually sufficiently impressive, even when discounted, to have a marked effect on his conduct for several hours there-after.

The power of the teacher and his aids extended even into the homes; our homework was closely supervised. When the weather was pleasant, we gathered on the roof-tops in the early evening and droned our lessons while two or three of the brightest pupils kept watch to be sure we weren't wasting our time or indulging in furtive tom-foolery. In winter, when we had to study inside, the watchers would steal up to the roof and listen down the chimneys for the telltale drone—or lack of it. To be caught not studying meant punishment the next day.

In spite of his strictness Elias Khoury was very popular with the children. On occasion he relaxed his dignity and played games with us in the *saha,* and sometimes he amused us with funny and interesting stories from the books he had read.

One day, several months after I had started at school, we were assigned to write a letter to the schoolmaster. "I want you to pretend," he said, "that it is ten years from now and you are living in some other part of the world. Write me a letter telling what you have been doing during that time, about the good and bad times you have been through, the adventures you have had, the new friends you have made, or anything else you might care to write about."

The pupils got out pencil and paper and set to work. They screwed up their brows as if in hard study, chewed their pencils thoughtfully, and looked out of the window for ideas. But I just sat. I had no paper. Noticing this, the schoolmaster gave me a sheet from his desk drawer. It was the first clean sheet of paper I had ever held in my hand. Before that I had practiced writing in sand, ashes, or dust, using my finger for a pencil. I now set to work excitedly, trying to get used to the thrill of my new writing tools, at the same time trying to compose a letter with one main idea: to express to my teacher my deep appreciation for all he had done for me.

That night he asked me to remain after school. I didn't remember having done anything bad, but then you never can tell. He had me sit down in front of him, and he looked at me for what seemed a long time without saying a word. I became uneasy. There were tears in his eyes. He shook his head. Then he said, "That was a very fine letter, Salom. I am glad you feel the way you do about me. You like school very much, don't you?"

"Yes, master," I said. "Someday I am going to be a priest."

"Yes, I know. George Nimur is a fine man, and if he says he will help you, he will help you."

"How did you know?" I asked, a little surprised to learn that he knew what I thought was a secret.

"He told me. He thinks you have promise. I think so, too. There are great things ahead for you, my son, great things—yes, greater even than you ever dreamed of—for, Salom, you are—a citizen—of America!"

I could not understand.

"Yes, Salom, you are a citizen—a citizen of America." He repeated the words slowly, as if helping me to taste their truth.

"I am a citizen of America! What do you mean, America?"

"You know what America is." He paused and looked at me and yet not at me but through me, as if into a great distance. "No—you don't know what it is. America, Salom," and he sighed deeply, "America is—is heaven."

"America is heaven?"

"Yes, America is heaven. Your people are there. Your father and brothers are there. And I am going to see that you go there soon."

I could not believe my ears. I am a citizen of America. America is heaven. My people are there. My schoolmaster will see to it that I go there soon. It was more than my poor little brain could grasp.

I plagued my schoolmaster with questions.

"But America is a country like Syria, isn't it?"

"Yes, Salom, it is a country—but not like Syria. It is really a country like heaven, and you cannot know what it is like until you have been there. And I have been there. I met your father there before you were born.

"When I came back here after the war to teach in this school, I didn't know you existed. When I asked you to come to school, and you told me you had no father and mother, I was not surprised. The war made many orphans. But when you said your name was Rizk, that set me to thinking. Who were your people? I asked questions about you. I found out that your mother died giving you birth. I knew that she was an American citizen. I learned that your brothers, who were born in America, had come here with your mother, and that they had been sent back to live with your father in America when your mother died. But you were kept here—by your grandmother Kbashy. Your grandmother did not want you to know about America. She had three sons, one of them your father, and America had taken them all away. So she never told you."

"But, master, am I really an American?"

"Yes. I have no doubt of that. You see, I knew that your brothers were Americans, and I thought that if they were

Americans you ought to be one, too. But I couldn't be sure. Maybe you weren't. Your brothers had been born in America, but you were born here. That might make a difference. So I checked up, and I find it is true. You are an American citizen. America is your rightful home. You belong there, and you ought to go there."

"You knew all this for a long time and didn't tell me?"

"I didn't want to tell you until I was sure. If I told you and it turned out to be wrong, you would be badly disappointed. I wanted to spare you that."

Then I asked him many questions, and he told me many more things about America which filled me with a growing delight and wonder. A slow light grew in my mind, as a night fire fed with wood grows bigger and bigger till you can see a great, bright circle of earth in the darkness. I could see America growing, rising, looming out of my ignorance, thrusting its huge continental shores, its mountains and forests and cities, out of the fog that was in me.

So many wonderful, unbelievable things my schoolmaster told me . . . the land of hope . . . the land of peace . . . the land of contentment . . . the land of liberty . . . the land of brotherhood . . . the land of plenty . . . where God has poured out wealth . . . where the dreams of men come true . . . where everything is bigger and grander and more beautiful than it has ever been anywhere else in the world . . . where wheat grows waist high, shoulder high, sky high, and as thick as the hair on your head . . . where mountains press their snowy heads against the sky . . . where forests teem with trees as plentiful as the sands of the sea . . . where men do the deeds of giants and think the thoughts of God . . . where they harness rivers of water to turn great machines and drench the land with light . . . where merely the push of a button does the work of thousands of horses and donkeys and camels and men . . . and schools . . . schools everywhere, in cities, in towns, in villages, and even where there are no villages . . . where everybody has a chance to learn, even the humblest child of the humblest Syrian immigrant . . . where there are medals and honors and prizes waiting to be won . . . where every boy and girl can learn to be what he or she wants to be . . . and more about schools and mountains and rivers and plains and cities. . . . Now it grew too big, too miraculous, too heavenly. It sounded like the fairylands my grandmother used to tell about, and I knew there were no more fairylands and no more fairies. But I wanted to believe all this, I had to believe it, and I did.

"When can I go there?" I cried.

"As soon as we can get word from your brothers, Salom. As soon as you can get a passport."

"What is a passport?"

"In this case, my son, it is a piece of paper that will let you into heaven on earth."

How wonderful! How beautiful! Like the magic lamp of Aladdin. Just a piece of paper, but it will open up the gates of heaven—my passport to paradise. I must write to my brothers at once. They will answer. They will tell me what to do. Then I will go to America—to heaven!

CHAPTER V

Land of My Dreams

ON ONE OF THE HILLS above Ain Arab and scattered down its slopes are the ruins of an ancient castle. You would never have guessed that these broken, weathered stones were once the stout walls of a king's fortress. You would have to be told, and then you might not believe it—not unless you happened to know that Syria is as full of old ruins as a graveyard is of tombstones.

There were stories about our old ruins to stir the imagination. We children used to play among them, and when we played, they became castles again, full of many rooms, hidden chambers, and secret passageways. When the game was war, the castle became our fortress. It was impregnable. Those in possession of it could not be dislodged; they could not be driven forth; they could not be sieged out; for, according to an old legend, a long, long cable stretched from the topmost tower of this castle to the temple towers of

Baalbek, eighty or so miles to the northeast. The legend said that the kings of the two towers used this wire to exchange gifts of clothing, jewelry, and food, safe beyond the reach of the thieves and robber bands which infested the hills between. So when we were in possession of the castle, we wined and dined in undisturbed luxury, never hungering or thirsting for anything, while the enemy outside fainted and perished for lack of food and water.

Many times I climbed to the top of the hill, sat in the shaded corner of a stone wall, and dreamed about America. Somehow those crumbled stones came to stand for all the strange and beautiful things I had heard and come to believe about my country—and what I believed about it was no less fantastic than what people believed about this ancient castle at my back.

When you come to think about it, it is really hard to tell what we did believe. We people of the Orient have a habit of exaggeration which frequently puzzles or disconcerts our more prosaic Western neighbors. We use exaggeration, not to lie, but to tell you how truly terrible or wonderful a thing seems to us. We are more interested in feelings than in facts, more interested in conveying an impression than in giving a report. If a hundred men engage in a battle we may describe it as a contest of thousands. We do not consider that padding the figures; we are only trying to give you a picture of how fiercely a hundred men fought. We are an imaginative people, a poetic people, a people of dreams, passions, wild fancies. You cannot even be invited into a Syrian home for dinner without being told, as likely as not, that the house is yours to burn, the children are yours to be sacrificed for your pleasure, and (in spite of this invitation to arson and murder) the day is blessed beyond compare because of your presence. You are not really expected to burn the house or do away with the children; this is only our way of telling you how welcome you are.

So when I say that it is really hard to say what we did believe about America, I mean that while the beautiful poetry about it conveyed to us a reality we could not have understood any other way, it also served to confuse and mislead us. At least it meant confusion and error to me.

Anyway, when I sat on that hilltop alone and remembered all the things my schoolmaster said and all the things the other people said about the most blessed land on earth, my imagination was free to roam and build without restraint or limit. Off to the west were the barren rolling hills. Somewhere beyond them, through the blue mist that covered their tops, was my home, my country. How wonderful it would be to wave one's hand, perhaps just to rub an Aladdin's lamp, lift the curtain of mist and behold the wealth and splendor of that paradise, or maybe sail right into it on a magic carpet.

You can imagine, too—no, you cannot imagine—the things I remembered and the dreams I dreamed, sitting in that castle corner. America was heaven, of course. That was the beginning. And the first thing about this heaven was the schools my teacher had told me so much about; the marble palaces of learning, some of them laid out like great cities in a magnificent oasis of green trees, grass, and flowers; where thousands of young men and young women were strolling on the grass, studying in the buildings, searching the heavens and the earth for knowledge and wisdom; where palatial buildings with more rooms than there were houses in Ain Arab were filled with endless rows of books and papers waiting to be read by eager students, scholars, wise men; where prizes, honors, and scholarships awaited those with talent and ambition; where every boy and girl, no matter how poor, could learn to read and write and be what he or she wanted to be— teacher, doctor, lawyer, priest; where there was no limit to how far you could go and how rich you could get if you were only willing to work and study. And the second thing was the abundance of everything that men desire of food and clothing and houses, of warmth and comfort, of richness and softness; so much wheat that you could bury all of Mount Hermon and all the hills around in an avalanche of golden kernels; so many cattle that if they were all rolled into one big animal, his nose would be in Beirut and his tail in Damascus. And the third thing was the peace of villages and cities that were never raided, looted, and terrified by arrogant soldiers and officials; where there were no wars, fears, and hates to keep the people in terror, to wreck their homes, destroy their crops and drive them weeping into the wilderness; where Christians do not sharpen the sword against the Mohammedans, but people of different religions live together in friendliness and peace; where men did not have to walk to the fields or go on journeys armed with rifles, knives, or swords. There were many, many things like that, so many it would take almost a whole book to write them down; for the America my schoolmaster painted for me was everything that my present life was not.

After a while my schoolmaster went away, and a new one came to take his place. Our new teacher had never been to America, so he could not answer all the questions which kept bursting into my mind.

With my old schoolmaster gone, I went to the hill more often than ever. Whenever my spirits were low, when I was disgusted with the sweat and drudgery of the fields, with their hot stones and piercing thorns and scratchy thistles, when poverty and hunger stared me in the face, when I could no longer bear the taunts and beatings of the bullies and tough guys, when my work kept me out of school for days on end, whenever anything went wrong at all, I would steal up to the castle alone and revel in the way things would be when I reached America.

With the help of my schoolmaster I had written a letter to my brothers in America. Then came weeks and months of waiting. There was no answer. The man came once a week with the mail, and every time he came I almost fell over myself trying to reach him first. But the letter did not come, and my disappointment was keener than I can describe. What had happened? Why didn't they answer? Hadn't my letter reached them? Had it been lost on the way? Or did they think I was a fake, using a clever lie to get to America?

I would see the mail man coming way up the trail, his long, dangling legs hugging his little donkey. I would scramble up to him excitedly and yell:

"No letter for me?"

"No. No letter for you."

"Are you sure there is no letter for me?"

"Of course I am sure."

"Will you please look again?"

"I don't have to look. There is no letter for you."

"When will my letter come?"

"I don't know. I'm not God."

He was exasperated. So was I; and disappointed, too, and crushed. And it happened to me once a week, week after week, for months. Every week my hopes would rise; and every week they would fall. Sometimes I talked to George Nimur; but even he was not as much comfort as my hill.

Then, after almost six months of agonized waiting, a letter came, the first letter I had ever received in all my life. Suddenly I stood out as a person set apart from the other villagers, somebody who counted. It was as if I had been in a great multitude of people and someone had risen and pointed a finger straight at me and said, "You are the one."

"Salom has a letter from America," somebody shouted. I almost choked from excitement. I couldn't wait. I grabbed the letter and ran, my throat throbbing, my veins full of fire; I ran among the buildings, clutching the letter to my ribs. Breathless, I stopped behind a house, fumbled at the flap, inserted my finger in one corner carefully, trying to open that precious envelope without tearing it. But I had to tear it. I unfolded the pretty paper I found inside, the beautiful magic paper—and my face fell. I couldn't read it. It was written in strange letters of a kind I had never seen before. I was almost disappointed enough to break into tears.

Now I ran back, fearful, bewildered, ashamed, and hopeful. I took the letter to our new schoolmaster. He couldn't read it, either! O God, how cruel the world is!

You have the most wonderful letter in the world, the first letter you ever received, and nobody can read it. Nobody can tell you what it says, whether to come to America at once or to stay in Syria forever.

The schoolmaster looks at me sympathetically. He looks at the letter again, removes the top page, and then breaks into a smile. "You can read this, Salom," he says, and he shows me the page.

Why, yes, the second page is Arabic. So are the third and fourth.

"Oh, thank you, thank you. Please, master, please, will you read it to me?"

My heart pounds frantically, my life is suspended in midair—and he reads.

My brothers are very, very surprised to learn I am alive and well. They can hardly believe it; yet they do believe it. They have no doubt of it. There is a little joke in the letter. They said that when my letter arrived, Uncle Gibran had to read it to them because they couldn't read Arabic. When my brother Charlie learned of my existence, he expressed amazement. He said, "But I thought he was dead. How come he wasn't killed?"

"Maybe he wasn't worth killing," my uncle said.

They put that in the letter. It was the truth. I wasn't worth killing. There were others, grown men, leaders of the people, men of thought and action who urged the people to rise against their oppressors, with speeches and with pamphlets which they secretly printed and distributed, and *they* were killed. They were men intoxicated with ideas, with dreams of peace and freedom and independence for themselves, their families, and their long-suffering people. They were bootleggers of freedom, of education and enlightenment, of truth and justice and the light of a new day. But Turkey had a prohibition against new ideas, against ideas which did not suit the regime; so those men were killed. But I was just a boy. I never made any speeches. I never protested. I meekly, ignorantly accepted the oppression and injustice, the poverty and misery. I really was not worth killing.

The letter went on to say that things were going well in America, that my brothers were working and making money, and that they were sending some of their money to the American consul at Beirut, telling him to find Salom Rizk, who was an American citizen, and instructing him to send me to America at once.

Well, they wouldn't have to find me. They wouldn't have to look any farther than the ends of their noses, because I was going to be there when they looked. I wasted no time in getting ready and saying good-by to my friends and relatives. They seemed to be as happy as I was that at last the dreams I had hoped for and despaired of a thousand times had come true. The loafers and even the town bully envied me. Just think, they said, Salom Rizk, that little ragged orphan, is going to America—and we have to stay here. I almost felt sorry to leave them.

Beirut was forty-five miles away. I covered the distance in less than three days, over weary miles of rocks, thorns, hot trails, and dusty roads. When I arrived, my legs were scratched and bleeding and the soles of my feet were hot and bruised as if they had been pounded incessantly with stones and pricked with a thousand needles.

It was almost night when I arrived in the city, which was big and dark, with a tangle of streets running in every direction; I was lost as soon as I entered.

I don't know where I slept that night. I think it was under somebody's porch; and I was so tired that I slept straight through until daylight. The first thing that popped into my head when I awoke was, "Soon, soon, I shall be in America. Today I shall get my passport; tomorrow, or maybe the next day, I shall go to America."

I was only fourteen years old then, and very, very ignorant about consuls and passports and ships to America.

CHAPTER VI

Disappointment at Beirut

How I EVER MADE MY WAY through the bewildering maze of streets and alleys, parks and squares, buildings and vehicles, people and animals that make up the city of Beirut is more than I know. But I did, and presently, by some miracle, found myself in the largest building I had ever been in. People were rushing to and fro, bumping into me—or maybe I was bumping into them, because there were so many marvelous things to behold I didn't have any eyes to see where I was going.

Everything I had seen as I inquired my way into the center of the city fascinated and frightened me. I almost forgot what I had come for. Time and again I stopped to gape at some strange new wonder: big, long, many-windowed vehicles rolling down the middle of the street on long, steel tracks, grinding to a stop and spewing out of their ugly mouths all kinds of funny-looking people;

men balancing precariously on two wheels and pumping their legs up and down for dear life, and then gliding down the street like statues; automobiles making a horrible noise and darting in and out among huge carts, wagons, and carriages drawn by horses, donkeys, and goats. Then there were beautiful, unveiled women with bright red faces and lips, and their robes were cut off at the knees, and some of them were pulling or being pulled by the most beautiful dogs I had ever seen. And tall buildings that shaded the streets from the sun; and, in the center of the city, a lovely garden of flowers, green grass, and big trees; and altogether such a mixture and jumble of swift-moving impressions that it was impossible to make order or sense out of them.

And now I was in the American building. Such elegance and beauty I had never seen before. The place fairly glittered. In my rags I felt as out of place as a beggar in a palace. I saw many people in native Syrian dress, and others wearing European clothes. I saw a picture of George Washington draped with an American flag. I knew it was George Washington, because it was just like the picture on the postage stamps of my letter.

After waiting for what seemed ages, I finally stood before a man wearing European clothes who spoke perfect Arabic. He eyed me strangely.

"And what can I do for you?" he asked.

"I want to go to America," I said. "I am an American citizen."

"Do you have your passport?"

"No. That is what I came to get. I have a letter from my brothers in America. They said they would send you money for my ticket."

"Do you have the letter with you?"

"Yes sir," I said, reaching into my rags and drawing forth my precious, dirty envelope. He reached for it, and I gave it to him. He read it carefully, put it down on a desk, and then said, "Will you please wait a minute?"

He went through a door, and I waited. Presently he came out, shaking his head. He said there was no letter and no money for me from America. He asked me where I lived.

"Ain Arab," I said.

"Where were you born?"

"Ain Arab."

He looked at me dubiously. "And you say you are an American citizen?"

"Yes sir. My mother was an American."

"When were you born?" he asked.

"In the winter."

"What year?"

"I don't know. I think it was 1908—maybe 1909."

"Do you have a birth certificate?"

"A what?"

"A birth certificate."

I knew what he meant, but I could not believe he really meant it. A birth certificate—a paper to certify that I was born? I thought a moment and then said, "I do not have a birth certificate. I am poor. Maybe I am too poor to have a birth certificate. I was born without one; but I am born, honestly—I——"

"I don't mean that," he said, holding a smile back. "I mean we have to have some proof that you are Salom Rizk, the same Salom Rizk . . ."

His voice went on piling up a jumble of words, but I hardly heard them. I was too stunned to get it all. But the drift was plain. It was coming through to me that I wasn't going to get to America, that I couldn't prove who I was or why I ought to go. In that moment the world seemed to heave, grow dark, dissolve under my feet. Everything was unreal—the long-ago words of my schoolmaster; the dreams that had seemed so real ever since; the letter I held in my hand; the words the man spoke to me now; the building I was in—all seemed like objects, figures, and words seen and spoken in a beautiful dream that had turned into a nightmare.

I stumbled out of the consulate and groped my way into the street through blinding tears.

Late that afternoon I stood on the doorstep at my aunt

Miriam's. She had been in Ain Arab once to visit us. When she recognized me she gasped, "Salom Rizk! How did you get so dirty?"

"I don't know," I said, not too happily, "but I am never going to wash again—not until I get to America."

But, of course, I did. Aunt Miriam would never let me sleep on her beautiful clean mat with all that dirt on me and with all those lice in my clothes.

The weeks went by, the months went by, and still I was marking time in Beirut, with no more hope of getting to America than the first time I visited the consulate. But I kept going back just the same, merely to insist that I was Salom Rizk, an American citizen. It all seemed useless. Always the answer was the same: you have no proof. And so long as you have no proof, you stand no chance of going to your country.

Two years go by—and still the same fruitless visits to the American building. I begin to doubt that I am Salom Rizk. Perhaps I am, after all, only a nameless orphan. Perhaps I have no family in America and no claims upon that country. When such doubts and fears plague me I try to fight them off by reminding myself of the words of my schoolmaster, the letters my brothers had written, the re-peated assurances of my friends in Kfer Kuk and Ain Arab that I am the son of Latefy Rizk who had lived in America.

To make that far-off land more real to myself, I would go to the American University in Beirut and stroll on the campus among the green trees, the vine-covered buildings, and the beautiful flower beds, imagining that I was no longer in Syria, but on real, honest-to-goodness American soil. Or I would visit the school's museum and imagine myself an American pupil studying the secrets of the bones and rocks in the glass cases. Sometimes a day of loafing and dreaming on the docks, watching the white sails drift lazily to and fro or, better yet, watching an occasional freighter steam off to the horizon, would restore my hopes. Yet, eating like acid at the back of my mind, in my heart, at the pit of my stomach was the terrible suspicion that I might not be an American. It was a dreadful thought, and I died a thousand deaths thinking it.

In the meantime I drifted aimlessly from one employment to another without ambition, without striving, without caring for any particular reward or success at any of them. My sole occupation was proving my citizenship. How could I be interested in anything else—in anything so dull as making a living? I worked indifferently, first as a baker's helper, then as errand boy, nursemaid, cabinetmaker's ap-

prentice, stableboy. Practically all my bosses regarded beating and kicking me around as one of the privileges of
employing me. It was very discouraging. After some time
I found myself employed as a glazier's apprentice. My boss
was a devout churchman and a hard-boiled slave driver.
Under his watchful eye you had to step lively, whether
repairing broken windows, fetching feed for his half-
starved donkey, or mopping the tile floors in his house.

Early one morning I went with him to repair some
windows in a tall building overlooking the Beirut harbor.
We had to start on the fourth floor, standing, at that dizzy
height, on the topmost rungs of a long ladder—a very
dangerous place.

At our back was the big blue sweep of the Mediterranean, with the fishing sails coasting like white shadows
on its ruffled surface, and stubby little tugs turning up
white furrows. Despite the danger I should like to have
sat there all morning with nothing to do but drink in the
peaceful beauty of the water and the lazy boats, but my
boss, being a practical man, would allow no daydreaming,
not even for a second. It was hurry, hurry all the time, so
I set to work almost furiously, scraping putty, pulling nails,
and enjoying the fresh clean tinkle of glass as it hit the
bricks below. Having removed all the broken glass, I had
just received a new pane from the hands of the boss when
a terrific blast rent the air. I was so startled I nearly fell

from the ladder. I grabbed for a rung, and the pane went hurtling to the ground, shattering into a thousand pieces. Feeling the ladder firm in my hands and solid under my feet, I looked around to locate the source of that fearful noise, and there, sliding into the harbor, graceful as a bird, was the largest, most beautiful ship I had ever seen. I had no sooner glimpsed it than my boss filled my ears with blood-chilling curses. After exhausting what was an extremely extensive vocabulary of profanity for a pious churchman, he told me to get out. "I never want to see your ugly face again," he bellowed. So far as I know, he hasn't.

It was the month of October in the year of 1925. Having just been relieved of my livelihood, I was again free to starve—and go where I pleased; so I thought to try my luck again with the American consul. I guess it was seeing that magnificent big boat that gave me the idea. It was on such a ship that one dreamed of crossing to America. But I never got to the consulate—not that time, and not for a long time after.

On my way I happened upon one of the most pitiful, heart-rending sights I had ever seen. An old Model T Ford drew to the curb just as I came up the street abreast of it. At the same instant that the car stopped, a woman screamed, half leaped, half threw herself to the pavement. Two men jumped from the car and raised her between them. She was sobbing wildly and beating her already bruised and swollen face with her fists. Over and over she cried, "My baby! My baby! O God, what have they done to my baby! O God, have mercy! O God, take vengeance!"

A crowd gathered at once and followed the men as they carried her into a near-by hotel.

Then it was that I learned the dreadful news. Damascus, that most beloved city of Syria, was being bombed by French planes and shelled by French guns.

Within a few hours I heard the story of the woman, and for days it seemed as if it were the only thing people could talk about. It seems this woman, a Mohammedan, was in bed recovering from childbirth when the battle of Damascus began. When the heavy shelling and bombing showed no signs of letting up—in fact, seemed to be getting worse— her husband and brother decided to move the family from the city at once and secured a dilapidated old Ford for the purpose. While the men were packing some of their effects, the mother rose from bed, wrapped her jewelry and a few other belongings in a blanket, grabbed her baby and ran out. Outside she saw soldiers approaching the car they were expecting to escape in. Afraid of losing her jewels, she ran to the rear of the house and threw the bundle into a well, expecting to recover it later. But later she discovered that the bundle she had tossed into the well was her baby.

In a short time the city was full of conflicting stories

about the trouble at Damascus. The bombing, rumor said, had lasted continuously day and night for almost three days. Whole sections alike had the very life pounded out of them. The streets were said to be strewn with dead and filled with cries of the wounded. People were fleeing for their lives in every direction. The rebels had barricaded themselves in the streets behind barbed wire, sandbags, furniture, and dead bodies. Hoping to intimidate them into submission, the French had tied the bullet-riddled bodies of twenty-five rebels to the backs of camels and paraded them through the streets of Damascus, later displaying them in the public square. The rebels were enraged, and the disorder spread. The French were helpless to control or subdue the situation—even with terror.

Later other stories of death and destruction came in. Outside Damascus scores of villages were being set upon by the Druses, who were at the bottom of the trouble. The roads were choked with refugees fleeing in all directions, some to Damascus, some toward Beirut, some toward Rasheiya, and others toward Baalbek. Trains were being derailed on the main road between Damascus and Beirut, the passengers robbed, stripped of every bit of clothing, and turned loose, naked, in the desert. Automobiles were stopped on the highway and turned over or commandeered by the fanatic rebel bands.

Although the Druse rebellion had broken out some

months before (in July, I believe it was), no one had expected anything like this, and no one had doubted the ability of the French authorities to control any situation. Our feeling of security had been further increased by growing signs of French military activity. Soldiers had landed from French ships at Beirut, marched through the streets in seemingly endless columns to tents on the edge of the city, rested for several days, and then marched on inland through the hills to the places of trouble. Tanks, huge guns, planes were unloaded, too, and driven or flown after the soldiers. But now it seemed all Syria had gone to pieces.

I began to fear for the safety of my grandmother, and sure enough within a few days word came that Ain Arab had been raided and its people either killed or driven out. I did not wait. I told my aunt I was going to Ain Arab at once and would be back in a few days, two weeks at most. She tried to dissuade me, but I felt I could take care of myself. Moreover, I believed that the worst dangers were past.

Nevertheless, I decided to avoid the main roads and trails as much as possible, either following them through the hills at a distance or taking short cuts on some of the less-used donkey trails. It was lucky that I did. Several times, when the going on the hills was rough, I descended to the main trail, and once I had to scurry behind a big boulder to keep out of sight of a Druse guerrilla band which showed evidence of having just raided a village. There must have been at least twenty of them, swarthy warriors and very fierce-looking with their fancy bandoleers, knife holsters, and long-barreled rifles. They rode on trim little Arabians, which straggled along like the beads of a broken necklace. Ahead of them they drove goats, cows, calves, and sheep. Behind them they dragged captured donkeys loaded with loot, sacks of squawking chickens, pots and pans, clothing, blankets and grain. I waited behind the boulder until they were out of sight and then proceeded cautiously down the road. Presently there came into view the villagers who had been set upon and driven out of their homes. They were a sorry-looking lot, most of them without shoes and insufficiently clad for the chilly weather. Mothers were carrying their babies; children toddled along, whimpering and crying. The men were carrying sacks apparently containing what little food they could scratch together after the raid. They didn't know where they were going.

I asked them if they knew anything about Ain Arab. Yes, they had heard it was raided and no one was there now. They thought most of the people had gone to Zahla.

So I went to Zahla, about fifteen miles north of Ain Arab. It was crowded with people who had fled from half a dozen villages near by. In spite of the terror and trials they had suffered they seemed very talkative and gay. The town had become an encampment. At night everybody slept in the houses, which were packed to the doors with rows of sleeping bodies. The men had knives and rifles and took turns standing guard day and night against surprise attack. In the surprise attack on Ain Arab, I learned, six of my relatives had been killed.

I found my grandmother staying in the house of a friend. "The Lord deliver me!" she exclaimed when she saw me. "What is this I see? I thought you were in America."

"No, not yet," I said. "Maybe not for a long time yet—but America is still in me."

We talked for a long time, and she told me how, by quick thinking, she had escaped possible death at the hands of the Druses.

"I tied their hands," she said.

"O Grandmother, you don't mean to say that——"

"Yes, I tied their hands—with my tongue. Do you remember when I went to Houran to get grain? I thank God a million times now that I went. On that journey I learned something about the Druses that works like a sacrament. They can be very cruel, very cruel, those Druses, but they are men of strict honor. If you know where their honor is, you can hold them down with a child's little finger. And I knew where their honor was. They surprised us in the morning, Sunday morning. We were at church. Before we knew what had happened they were on top of us. It was so quick the men didn't have time to run for their rifles. We were trapped. The priest said to be quiet, to stay where we were and keep a prayer in our hearts. Then he began to pray. But when I got a chance, I ran to the house."

"Why, Grandmother," I said, "you might have been killed."

"No, the Druses were mostly at the other end of the village. Besides, they don't bother the women much."

"But why didn't you stay in the church?"

"I had all my treasure at the house. I couldn't let them take the treasure."

"But what could you do about it?" I asked. "If the Druses want to take the treasure, they take it."

"Then you have to make them want not to take it. I waited in the house, and pretty soon a Druse came on horseback. I ran out and put my hand on his knee like this. Then I reached up and tied a knot in his *khafeya* like this. At the same time I cried, '*Beerthuk* [By the honor and virtue of your women]!' Just like that—'*Beerthuk!*'—and his hands were tied. A Druse would die a thousand times before he would violate the honor and virtue of his women. I learned that when I went to Houran. But his rage, you should have seen his rage because he could not take anything."

"But the other Druses, what about them?" I asked.

"I said the same thing to all of them—'*Beerthuk!*'" my grandmother replied, chuckling. "It is just like taking all their greed and all their weapons away. They are helpless as children."

"But the Druses destroyed the town anyway, didn't they?"

"Yes, they took almost everything. All day they looted the houses and gathered up the animals. At night they built fires to keep a watch on us, but some of us slipped away and ran through the night. It was dreadful. It was raining hard, and the hills were very slippery. We fell down a thousand times, so tired we felt like dying. But the men helped us, and in the morning we came to Aithi. We were a mess—mud from head to foot and almost too tired to talk. The people gave us food and dry clothes. We slept and then came to Zahla."

"Thank God you are alive," I said.

"Yes, thank God any of us are alive."

"How long are you going to stay here?" I asked.

"I don't know. When the danger is past we shall go back home."

"I'm afraid it won't be safe in Ain Arab for a long time. Why don't you come to Beirut? The Druses will never——"

"Beirut! Ach, we could never go to Beirut. The city is not for us. I am a farmer. You do not farm in Beirut. No, we shall go back to Ain Arab. This is not the first time we have been chased out of our houses, and it won't be the last time. If the Druses come again, I shall trust in God and shout 'Beerthuk!' That is better than a sword."

Satisfied that I could not provide any better protection than "Beerthuk!" I returned to Beirut. Tension and fear were everywhere. The Christians had lost confidence in the French government and began to fear that the Druses would overrun the country and drive out the French. In that event the Christians knew they could expect no mercy, for they had been supporting the French, even volunteering for service and organizing independent fighting units to help put down the rebels.

Certainly, if the rumors were to be believed, the rebellion was growing in extent and terror each day. More and more villages were being raided, travel was becoming more dangerous, Damascus was still an armed citadel; attacks, robberies, massacres were still on the increase.

One question that was on everybody's lips was, "Who is arming the Druses? Where do they get all the guns and ammunition?" People were saying, "Somebody is behind the Druses. Some great European Power is arming them. Who is it?" "It is England." "No, it is Germany." "No, it is Italy." Everyone seemed to have a different answer, and the strangest and most unbelievable of all was, "France is arming them." I talked to Frenchmen who took this for granted and even justified it.

In the hotel where I now worked, a youthful French civil

engineer, who had married a beautiful Syrian girl, told me, "Why, everybody knows the French are arming the Druses."

I couldn't believe it. "You mean the French government is stupid enough to give weapons to those who rebel against it?"

"No, no, not the French government, but French munitions makers—those who manufacture guns and bullets."

"But why doesn't the government put a stop to it? They can keep their own citizens from selling weapons to the enemies of France, can't they?"

"No, they can't, and if they could, what good would it do? There are English and Italian and Czech and American munitions makers. If the French did not sell them arms, somebody else would. Somebody is going to get this business, and it might as well be the French as anybody."

"But that is wrong," I cried. "Surely someone has the power to put an end to all this murder. Thousands of Syrians are dying. Yes, and French soldiers are murdered with their own bullets. People are suffering, innocent people, from hunger and cold. They are being driven from their homes like animals, driven out into the winter, with nothing to eat and nothing to wear. I have seen it with my own eyes. Yes, they have killed my own relatives—six of them. The Druses murdered them with French guns and French bullets."

"That is too bad," he said. "Too bad."

It began to appear that the war was going to get worse, much worse, and last a long time. In the harbor of Beirut I saw shiploads of soldiers arrive and march in what seemed further endless streams past the hotel where I worked. Fine, ruddy-faced poilus, Moroccans, Circassians, and Senegalese with their black, shiny faces and colorful uniforms, spahis with their fierce eyes and dashing capes, and the famous fighters of the French Foreign Legion. Always they came, more and more of them, until I thought they must inundate the very mountains of Syria. And they had fighting equipment the Druses never knew existed—long guns, heavy guns, machine guns by the hundreds, tanks which rumbled on the streets like thunder, armored cars with roaring motors; trucks and planes; and huge horses, the biggest I had ever seen, dragging supplies, load upon load. Every day I saw more soldiers and more war machines pouring through the streets and out over the hills— enough, I thought, to blow up all Syria and not leave one brick or stone on top of another. And every day the news became blacker and blacker. The French lose more ground, suffer more defeats, lose more soldiers, and the Druses come closer and closer to controlling all Syria.

How could that be? How could bands of barefoot, poorly armed peasant and primitive mountaineers win so many victories against the mightiest, most modern army in

Europe? What was wrong? Maybe the French munitions makers *were* arming the Druses with rifles. Yet how could even these fierce fighters stand against the tanks, artillery and machine-gun fire, the bombing planes, and trained soldiers of France?

My civil engineer friend explained that, too: "The Druses are smart fighters, and the French have a bad conscience."

"What do you mean, smart fighters? Do you mean the Druses are smarter than the French?"

"They are in their own way of fighting. The Druses are too smart to meet the French in mass battle. They know they wouldn't last an hour. That's why they have divided their forces into little guerrilla bands—not more than twenty-five to thirty men to a party. And those bands are scattered all over Syria. They hide in the hills, which they know like a book, and only attack when there isn't a French garrison or French troops within miles. Why, it keeps a whole battalion busy just figuring out what those rebels are doing. It's just like hunting rats. You can never get all of them. Besides, they have no heavy guns to slow them up. They have no plans except to harass the French out of Syria. All they have to do is to keep things in an uproar until the French are so sick of their mandate they will beg the League to take it back or give it to somebody else."

"But why don't the French fight the way the Druses do?

They can break up into small bands, too. And they have airplanes to see them from the air."

"Well, guerrilla fighting is only half of the story. The French don't have their hearts in this fight. There are plenty of Frenchmen in Paris who are sick of the whole mess already. They are blaming themselves and they are blaming the politicians and they are blaming Sarrail. They say that Sarrail does not understand the Syrian spirit, that he has undone all the fine work of Weygand. And the bombing of Damascus, they think, is inexcusable, horrible, thoughtless, brutal.

"You wait and see, there will be no end to this until either every last Frenchman has been driven out or every last Druse has been killed—and that will never happen."

If what the Frenchman said was true, Syria was in for a long siege of it. It might be years before things settled down again—and it might be never. It seemed to me then that we had never really known any peace, that there had always been blood and terror and homelessness and sorrow in the land, and there always would be to the very end of time.

My mind had been so completely absorbed with recent happenings that I had literally forgotten about America. Now I remembered it, more keenly than ever. I began to wish, hope, pray more fervently than words can describe that I might escape this eternal nagging poverty and fighting forever. But as they say, "If wishes were horses, beggars would ride"—and I was virtually a beggar.

CHAPTER VII

Five Bags of Gold

ALMOST FIVE YEARS since I first called at the American consulate, and still I was wasting precious time in Beirut. During all these months and years I alternated between the most violent moods of hope and despair. My brother continued writing letters, not very many, but enough to keep alive a small flame of hope, enough to keep the fluctuating temptation of America ever before me. "Be patient, Salom," he would write, "we are making progress and you ought to be in America in six months." Six months later a letter would come, saying, "Please do not give up, but we have run into difficulties. I can't say how long it will take." It was maddening. Time went on and on, and it was always the same old story—letters, words, promises, delays, and more delays—until I was more often sick at heart than not. A growing sense of futility and desperation was putting me in the mood for almost any adventure which might promise fulfillment of my dreams.

I had found employment doing odd jobs in an expensive hotel with a very high-sounding name—the Grand Hotel Victoria. It had twelve rooms. My duties were many— washing dishes and scrubbing floors, polishing silverware and brass ornaments, cleaning lamp chimneys and empty- ing spittoons and garbage pails, running errands for the boss and the hotel guests. I was what you call a "flunkey." My pay was meager, four liras a month, which is about three dollars in American money.

A smooth, cocky young fellow called Jaboor worked here, too, doing pretty much the same kind of work I did. He was always getting himself into trouble and talking himself out of it. Several years older than I, he was very much smarter and knew it. He was a Lebanese and had studied for the priesthood in a Jesuit seminary. There he had learned to speak French fluently and had picked up an immense and interesting knowledge of the world outside of Syria. I came to admire him greatly because of his self- confidence, easy swagger, and coolness under any kind of excitement.

Jaboor told me he had left the seminary to marry, but the girl's parents had disapproved of the match because of his poverty. His ambition now was to amass a fortune, marry another girl, and show those parents what a wonderful son-

in-law they had missed. Consequently he was always thinking up get-rich-quick schemes. Mostly, though, he never
got beyond stealing champagne from the hotel stocks and
short-changing the customers who sent him on errands to
near-by shops and drugstores.

Our errands frequently took us down a street which runs
diagonally from the seashore into the center of the city. I
got to know some of the vendors and craftsmen who sold
their wares and plied their trades on this street and to
exchange greetings with them. One day one of the shoemakers, a familiar figure in those parts, hailed me, "Are
you going by the liquor shop?"

"Yes sir," I answered.

"Well, come here. I want you to fetch me a bottle of
arrack," and he handed me a coin.

So I brought him his arrack, and that was the beginning
of a very strange and, as it turned out, a very fortunate
friendship.

Abdo was his name, or at least the only name he ever
gave me. After our first meeting I used to stop and talk
with him almost every time I had an errand on that street,
and pretty soon I was going down to see him afternoons
when I had a little time off. He was a very interesting and
exciting fellow, a sort of sinner-saint who had tasted all the
sins, pronounced them all bad, and kept on doing them.
He was gravely concerned that I should escape them all.

After vividly describing all the delights of some particular vice, he would roundly lecture me against it, detailing all the evil and loathsome consequences in the most hair-raising language. He had used opium and hashish and arrack, and frequented the brothels of Beirut and Haifa, Cairo and Alexandria as long as he could remember, and from them he had formed his cynical opinions of woman-kind in general.

He had no use for money and much less use for people who coveted it. He was a shoemaker by trade and an expert who was sought out by wealthy and particular people who paid fancy prices for his skill. It took him about two days to finish a pair of shoes, and he always charged enough so that he could live the rest of the week without working. No amount of money could induce him to make more than one pair of boots or shoes a week. He had a brother who was some sort of an official in the Greek Orthodox Church and who, on the side, had charge of renting church-owned properties in the shopping and tenement districts of Beirut. It made Abdo's blood boil to think of how his brother squeezed the little shopkeepers and the poor people in the tenements. "And don't think all that money goes to the church, either," he would say, emphasizing his point with a deafening blow of his hammer. Whenever he expressed contempt for anyone, he always said, "I hate him as if he were my own brother."

One day, a few weeks after I had met Abdo, I was on my hands and knees scrubbing the floor in a rear room of the hotel when the owner came in. Instantly he was in a rage.

"Where did you get that soap?" he shouted.

"The maid gave it to me."

"And you're scrubbing floors with it, you devil's apprentice. Don't you know soap is gold?"

By this time he was towering over me. He lifted his boot, and before I could get out of the way it crashed into my ribs. I rolled over, screaming, and sprawled on the floor as if felled with an ax. My wind was completely knocked out of me. Then came a hail of more blows falling so fast and furious that I couldn't get out of the way. I covered my head with my arms and yelled until the kicking subsided.

"You are through," the boss yelled. "And your back wages are just enough to pay for the soap you've wasted."

I had something like four or five dollars coming, so I began to appreciate the value of soap.

That night I went to see Abdo. I told him what had happened, and he was all for committing a murder on the spur of the moment. But after some reflection he decided to postpone it.

A couple of days later Jaboor hunted me up at the seaside and took me to one side. He looked very mysterious but wouldn't tell me anything except that he wanted me to come to the hotel that afternoon. I didn't have anything else to do, not having found another job yet, so I went.

He had told me to meet him in the rear entry, and that is where I found him. He was smoking a cigar butt evidently retrieved from a cuspidor.

"Do you want to get rich, very rich?" he asked me, in a deep whisper.

"Rich? Sure, I'd like to be rich, but how?"

"Never mind, I know how. I have a plan. Do you want to do it?"

"Do what?"

"Get rich, get rich!"

"Yes, but how?"

"It's easy. You know Nazeem Agha, the date merchant from Bagdad? He has five big leather bags in his room, and they are full of gold. They are in his room now. They are so heavy you can't even lift them."

"You mean those big leather bags have gold in them?" I had seen them in the date merchant's room and had been curious to know what was in them, but had never had the courage to inspect anybody's baggage. In fact, we had strict orders from the clerk never to molest the possessions of the guests, under penalty of dismissal.

"Do you want to see them?" asked Jaboor.

"I don't know."

"What's the matter? Are you afraid?"

"No, I'm not afraid. But you want me to steal."

"How else are you going to get rich?"

"I don't know, but I don't think we should steal to get rich."

"Listen, there's only one way to get rich, and that's to steal. This man has got so much money he'd never miss it. Besides, how do you think he got it? We can get a sack and take a little out of each of his leather bags, and he'll never know it until it's too late to find out who did it. Come on, I'll show you the gold."

"But what if we get caught in the room?"

"Aw, we won't get caught. He's sitting out on the balcony. He sits there all afternoon and smokes his pipe. Never looks right or left. He just smokes and snores. I've watched him."

I was still dubious, but I went. Anyway, it wouldn't hurt to see the gold. I had never seen that much gold in all my life.

We crept stealthily up the back way to the second floor and walked tiptoe down the carpeted hall. The date merchant was sitting out on the balcony overlooking the Mediterranean. We could see the back of his head. He had guests, and they were talking. My heart began to pound, and suddenly I began to think of what it would be like to be shot. How does a bullet feel? What happens when you die? What do you do when you get caught snooping around in other people's possessions? My skin became wet and sticky. My ears were suddenly sharpened to the tiniest noises, and every step we took threatened to sound like the footfall of a giant. I don't think I breathed the whole length of the hall. When we made the room, Jaboor turned around and looked at me. He snickered.

"You're scared," he said.

"Aren't you?"

"No."

"What if we get caught?"

"If you hear somebody coming, you start straightening things up. I'll pretend I'm wiping dust from the floor. See, I've got a rag," and he pulled a dirty cloth from somewhere. "You stand there by the door and just sort of listen. If you hear anything, give me a signal and then get busy."

So I stood there listening and looking around the room for something to straighten up if we should be surprised. When I realized that everything was in perfect order, my heart was in a panic. Jaboor was down on his knees and began to fumble with the strings on one of the leather bags. Pretty soon he had the bag open, and he motioned for me to come.

What a sight to behold! Beautiful, shining, round gold pieces, thousands of them.

Jaboor reached into the bag, drew out a coin and handed it to me.

"Feel it," he whispered. "You could live a whole week on one of them, and you could live like a king. No more work in no damn hotel. Hell, you could be a hotelkeeper yourself and kick everybody around and have lots of fun—women and everything."

I handed back the coin. "We better get out of here."

"Wait a minute," he said. "See if you can lift one of them."

"Don't you think we better go?"

"Naw, wait a minute, just lift one of them."

So I took hold of a bag and lifted. It came off the floor all right, but it was heavy. There must have been nearly sixty pounds in each sack.

We started toward the door, made the hall, and sneaked back down the back way just as we had come up. At the bottom, Jaboor stopped. I breathed more easily, but my heart was still pumping hot blood all over me.

"Now listen," Jaboor said. "Tonight I'll get a bag. Then tomorrow night I'll meet you at the Crown and we'll come over here. You'll go down into the court and hide in the bushes under the window. I'll go up to the room and drop a bag out. But you don't move—not yet. You wait five minutes, and if nobody comes, it's safe. When you hear me whistle, you bring the bag to the gate. I'll meet you there with a cart. Then we'll hide it and I'll come back to the hotel. They'll never guess I had anything to do with it. Smart, isn't it?"

I went to see Abdo at once. He was still working on that week's pair of shoes, working away happily and humming some sailor's tune to himself. I told him about Jaboor's scheme.

"Don't you have anything to do with it," he cried when he understood what we were up to. "You'll get caught and sent to prison."

"But, Abdo," I said, "Jaboor says we can't get caught."

"No, he can't get caught, but you can. Listen, do you know how much noise a big bag of gold makes when it drops fifty feet?"

"No, do you?"

"Well—no, but I'll bet it will make a hole in the ground ten feet, and make a noise like a French cannon. Why, the whole city of Beirut will hear the report. And the police and all the hotel will come running. And where will you be? Hiding in the bushes. And where do you think the police will look first? In the bushes. And what will you say? 'Oh, I was picking some berries for a *fatyer!*' And then they will send you to prison, and you will stay there till you rot. No sir, you stay away from that Jaboor. He is *afreet*—a master devil!"

"But just think, Abdo, there are five big bags—five big bags of real gold. I had some in my own hands."

"Listen, you put this out of your heart. You are not going to be a thief. I'll tie you to this bench, I'll throw you in the sea, but you are not going to steal." He paused a moment, spat vehemently at a fly, and then asked, "Where would you rather go—to prison or to America?"

"To America, of course. But think of it, Abdo, if I get money maybe I can go to America. Maybe I can buy my way. Besides, I'm tired of being poor and getting kicked around all the time. I just work and work and work and get no place, and I wait and wait and wait, and still America is as far off as ever. If I had gold, I could get to America."

"If you steal," Abdo said, and his face was full of dark menace, "if you steal, you will never get to America. America does not take people with a bad character. America is good. America is clean. It does not want thieves and murderers. If you get caught—and you will get caught— there will be no America for you. There will be prison, that's all. Now forget it."

Abdo leaned over his shoes and worked with all the intentness of a man trying to help somebody else forget something. I watched him and pondered his words.

After some time he said, speaking aloud to himself, "Five bags of gold. Five bags of gold. That is no job for boys. That's for men, real men. I wonder how you would go about it."

"Go about what?"

"Stealing five bags of gold. No, no, not you, not you.

This is not for boys, not for boys. This takes thieves, expert thieves."

After further meditation he said, "I know! Elias Aleppy! Yes, Elias Aleppy. He would be just the one. He hates the rich, too. He would be glad to do it—glad to rob the robber. But how shall I reach him?" Abdo fell into deep thought. He filled his mouth with tacks and hammered away. When his mouth was empty, he said, "Maybe you could take him a message, Salom."

Take Elias Aleppy a message! . . . The great, gallant, Christian gangster—the Robin Hood of Christian Syria! How wonderful, how thrilling! I had seen him once at a church festival—St. Nicholas Day, I think it was—over at the great Greek convent in the sand hills south of Beirut. I was surprised when I had seen him. I had always thought of him as a great, fierce man, but he was a little old fellow, humble, tame-looking, almost saintlike, with a very crinkly, kindly face. He was so poor he had to bum cigarettes from the other celebrants. Yet he had stolen fabulous sums of money in his lifetime, enough to be one of the richest men in Syria—and horses and cattle and sheep and goats and fruit and grain. Stealing with Aleppy was a principle. He robbed and raided to even up the scales of justice. Whenever a band of Turkish soldiers or tax collectors stripped a Christian village, he would retaliate by looting a Mohammedan village. The loot he gave to the raided Christians, who hailed him as a hero and a saint.

So now I was to carry a message to the great Aleppy; what a thrill went down my back!

Just then Abdo said, "No, you better not go. You have to keep out of this; we can't let you get mixed up in anything like this."

While Abdo was busy hatching plans to get the date merchant's gold, Jaboor appeared. Abdo made short work of him.

"Get out of here, you devil's bastard. Don't ever show your face here again."

And Abdo's face was so fierce that Jaboor lit out of there as if frightened by a bear.

Two days later Jaboor came back. He was a sight. His face was streaming blood. His eyes were black and puffy, and he was limping badly. Abdo tried to clean him up, but when Jaboor started to tell what had happened Abdo became worried and told him to beat it before he got us into trouble, too. He hadn't gone five hundred feet down the street before the police seized him. We learned later that he had been sent to prison. I shudder even now to think what a close shave I had. Without Abdo to restrain me, I don't know whether I would have joined Jaboor in his scheme or not. I am glad though that Abdo took me under his wing and kept me from falling into the clutches of a strange and tempting city like Beirut.

CHAPTER VIII

My Home, My Native Land

AFTER THE LONG MONTHS AND YEARS of waiting the great day came. The man at the consulate gave me my passport and congratulated me. "I am glad to know," he said, "that you really are Salom Rizk."

"I knew it all the time," I told him.

Bursting with joy, I raced from the American building to spread the good news to my friends.

Within a few days I stood on the quay saying good-by to Syria, perhaps never to see it again. I remember the kisses and the tears, the well-wishes and God-bless-yous, the little gifts, the joking and laughter—Abdo cutting capers to keep the tears back, my aunt Miriam telling me whom to see in America and what to tell them.

I remember the harbor of Beirut slipping away and fading into the sea; and my going to my cabin and crying, forgetting all the misery and hunger, the kickings and beatings, the wandering and the loneliness, and recalling only the good friends and good times I was leaving behind.

I remember my cabin mate, a very religious fellow, who would dangle a rosary from the porthole when the seas were rough; and how, when he once left the porthole open after quieting a storm with a medallion of St. Christopher, a huge wave washed in and flooded the cabin, and how two angry stewards mopped up the mess and threw the medallion into the sea.

I remember the long days, the endless, endless days of water, when it almost seemed that America had sunk into the sea and we were lost forever in an infinite expanse of blue.

And I remember hearing, from my cabin below, the sudden shouts on the deck, the running of feet, and the heavy stir which announced the first sight of American shores. I remember crowding to the rail and seeing a dark mass on the horizon, the sharpening outlines of things; the great tall lady with the flaming torch; the immigrants pressing the rail and shouting deliriously, cheering the statue as if it were a living thing which heard and responded to their wild and childish greetings.

And I remember the feelings, the anxious thoughts, the flood of questions which crowded into my mind: "O God, am I really here? Is this my home, my native land? Will I be able to make it? Fit in? Feel right? Act right?"

A strange feeling of belonging nowhere, of being suspended between two worlds, swept over me: I had left one world, I had not yet arrived in the other; I was lost.

Then I remembered my little bundle with all my worldly possessions tied up in it. I ran down to the cabin to get it, while Abdo's words rang in my ears: "America does not take people with a bad character. . . . America is clean." As I returned to the deck, a prayer of resolve, which I wanted above all else to keep, rose up in my heart: "O God, let me enter my country with a clean heart and a clean soul and a clean mind. Let the ocean swallow all the bitter memories, the doubts and hatreds and fears. Let me enter worthy of America, worthy of all that she stands for."

New York City was overwhelming, an unbelievable jumble of swiftness and bigness—millions of people, millions of cars, buildings, windows, lights, noises—a great mass of vagueness swimming and spinning in my eyes, too wonderful and too dazzling for me to see in part or understand as a whole. Still dazed with admiration and burning with questions, not one of which I could ask, because I knew no word of English, I was put on a train and rushed to the Middle West.

Did I say rushed? Well, yes and no. The train sped with such incredible speed for so long that it seemed we must be going around the world; yet time passed so slowly that I could hardly remember when I had not been on this train.

We had not been riding more than half a day before I began to pester the conductor with efforts to leave the train. He persuaded me to stay. The train rolled on and on. At almost every stop I asked the conductor, "Sioux City?" and he shook his head. My uneasiness mounted, but he only kept stretching his arms out wide to indicate a long, long distance yet to be traveled.

Several seats down and across the aisle from where I sat, I overheard a woman speaking my language. My hopes lifted. I walked over to her seat and said, "I am just new in the country. I cannot speak English to make the man understand where I want to get off. Maybe you could help me?"

"Ach," she said, "maybe you could help *me*. I cannot speak English, either."

After a while she got off in a big city and I did not even have the consolation of someone to share my predicament.

But I did not spend all my time trying to get off at different stations. Imagine my wonder and astonishment at the richness and beauty of the countryside, the splendor and magnificence of the cities. It was early summer. The country was bursting with green abundance. Everywhere were rich farm estates, each one like a kingdom, each farmer like a king. And everywhere were the animals, thousands of them, horses and cows and pigs and chickens.

The cows especially interested me. How big and healthy they looked, how sleek and fat! Instead of running themselves ragged hunting a few spears of grass, as the Syrian cows do, these cows were actually taking life easy in deep, green pastures, grazing lazily on the hillsides or lying contentedly under the shade of great trees. Whenever I saw a large aggregation of cattle, I thought they were the community herd. Later, when I learned they all belonged to one farmer, I was inclined not to believe it.

The great green fields stretched out and rolled on and on as far as the eye could see, and everywhere were magnificent groves of tall trees. When I saw all this rich beauty, I repeated to myself a million times, it seems, "Now, now at last I shall be free from poverty forever, free from poverty in America."

On and on the train thundered, through the first day and into the night, and out of the night into the day. The sights and sounds repeat themselves over and over, endlessly, like a snatch of song caught in the head: the small towns the train disdains; the big cities which it honors with a stop; the large rivers and vast plains; the horses and cattle and pigs and chickens; the tremendous tangle of railroads in every city; the monstrous manufacturing plants with their hundreds of smokestacks blowing up clouds that were like the portents of a storm; and the huge fields filled and packed with motorcars—cars, cars, and more cars, parked, crawling, speeding, shooting under bridges, over bridges, turning, twisting, racing the train, stopped by the train— millions of them. And millions of them piled up, broken and smashed, in fields outside the cities. America! Immense, beautiful, rich, wonderful, prodigal America!

And here I am still on the train with its endless puffings, its blowing of whistles and ringing of bells, twisting around curves, shooting over rivers, crawling over mountains, tearing across the plains, madly devouring the country—and always the conductor insists that I stay on. Pretty soon we would reach the last border of the continent; then he would tell me he forgot to let me off. What would I do then? I was sure I did not have enough money to buy back all that distance we had left behind.

Then, at last, Sioux City. Out of the train and into a taxi, twisting and whirling and careening through the streets, missing death and destruction by inches at almost every turn. We stop in front of a big white house with boxes of flowers under the windows. I have no sooner climbed out of the cab than a dark, buxom woman comes running down the steps with her arms flung wide. She throws them around me and hugs me so tight I grunt. This is my aunt, and that is her greeting. I look at her. I look at the house. Just for an instant I have the feeling toward her that the poor people in Syria have in the presence of the rich and great. And then she says something that gives the perfect touch to my whole experience of America up to that moment. She gives me the warmest of all welcomes: *"Ya meet ahla wsahla!"*

The warmth and hospitality of those words cannot be put into any other language. Literally, they mean, "The people and the plains are yours." I had heard them countless times in Syria, almost as many times as we had guests, but now they took on a new and richer meaning. The people and the plains are yours—yes, and the cities and the farms and the mountains and the rivers and the lakes and the forests, all the richness and beauty and splendor of America are mine now and forever. I am not ashamed to say that tears streamed down my face when I felt the full meaning and glory of that. The people and the plains are yours . . .

We entered the house, and I said, "But where is Uncle? Where is Charlie? Where is Joe?"

My aunt laughed. "Uncle is working. Charlie and Joe don't know you're coming. We kept it for a surprise. Charlie can't read Syrian, you know, and when your letter came telling us you were coming, we read Charlie everything except that part. Tonight we are going to have a big party, and then you will see Charlie."

"What a beautiful house you have, Aunt Athena! Uncle must be a very wealthy man."

"Oh no, Salom, he is not a wealthy man, but we get along very well."

"Where is Uncle?" I asked.

"He's at the meat-packing house."

"At the meat-packing house. Does he own a *muslach* [slaughterhouse], my good uncle?"

My aunt laughed heartily at that. "No, no, Salom. All Syria is not rich enough to own a packing house. A packing house is a huge industry where four thousand or more people work. They slaughter and prepare thousands of animals every day, and they ship them all over the world. I wouldn't be surprised but what they even send meat to Syria."

"What does Uncle do in the packing house?"

"Ugh," she said, "he skins cattle. It is hard work, not very pleasant."

"But, Auntie, how could all this be? Uncle, you say, is only a workingman who skins cattle, and he lives in such a house! I don't understand. How can——"

"Yes, and he owns it, too," my aunt said with pride. "Thank God, we don't have to pay rent."

"But where did Uncle get all the money to buy a house like this, and send so much to his mother and brother in Syria, and bring two sisters to America besides? Can one workingman do all that in America?"

"Oh yes, and make a good living, too."

"May Allah bless it," I said.

"America is all right, if you are willing to work, but it's no place for loafers," my aunt said. "Excuse me, Salom. I want to call your uncle."

Then I was introduced to the telephone. My aunt removed a bell-shaped object from a hook on a box suspended from the wall, turned a perforated disk several times and then said hello and something about Mike Gibran in English. Motioning me to her side, she said, "Salom, you talk to him."

"But, Auntie, I can't speak English," I protested.

"You don't have to speak English, Salom," she said, laughing.

"You mean this machine speaks Syrian, too."

"It speaks any language, Salom. Just hold the receiver up to your ear. When Uncle says hello, answer him."

Just then a faraway voice said, "Hello, Mike Gibran speaking."

"Hello, *Khally*," I said excitedly. "I am here."

"Hello, Salom," he cried, and his voice was full of joy and excitement. *"Ya meet ahla wsahla!"* There it was again —the people and the plains are yours!

"How are you, Salom?"

"Fine."

"How was the trip?"

"Wonderful."

"Tell Auntie I'll be home just as soon as I can."

About forty families came that evening to the big party my aunt had planned. Everybody was eager for news from the folks in Syria. How is my mother? How is my father? How are my brothers, sisters, uncles, aunts, cousins, nephews, nieces, grandparents? It seemed strange. Here I was in the heart of America, and we spent almost the whole evening talking about the old country.

My brother Charlie, not suspecting anything, had gone to an early movie. When he finally arrived, it was all I could do to pretend I wasn't there. And when he spied me —well, we just fell into each other's arms and wept like mothers over their long-lost children. I could not remember him, but he said he had vague recollections of me before he had been brought back to America as a boy.

The next day I went to visit my aunt Frieda. After we had talked ourselves out, she went to a cabinet in the corner of the room, turned a knob, and then stood smiling at me. Shortly a horn on the cabinet crackled and spat. "Static," she said, stooping over and manipulating more knobs. Presently music and voices poured forth.

"What is it?" I asked. "A phonograph?"

"No, Salom, this is a radio."

"What's a radio?"

"It's a wireless instrument for receiving music, news, and stories from far away."

"Is it like Aunt Athena's telephone?"

"Something like it, but the telephone uses wires. This doesn't."

"Does the radio speak Syrian, too?"

"Sure, Salom, it speaks any language. Whatever you say into it comes out of it."

"Could I speak into it?"

Aunt Frieda laughed. I was leading her a merry chase with all my curious questions. She had to explain to me how the very air in the room where I stood was full of the most interesting programs of music, stories, and news sent out by stations hundreds of miles away, and how by turning the dials on the box in her house you could pick out any program you wanted.

It was incredible and marvelous—like Alladin and his magic lamp. When I understood the purpose of the radio, I literally danced around it with joy. I thought, "If I cannot go to school at once, I can get my education over this little miracle machine. All I have to do is to learn English, and a whole new world of knowledge and understanding will be at my finger tips."

Ya meet ahla wsahla—the people and the plains are yours! How rich with new meaning those ancient words of welcome had become—as if all of America, body and spirit, had been poured into them.

CHAPTER IX

Adventures in a Slaughterhouse

THOSE FIRST FEW DAYS in America were all I had dreamed and more. Almost the first thing my brothers did was to take me downtown to a clothing store and fix me up from head to foot with a new American suit, new American shirts, ties, hat, shoes, and socks. They even changed my name from Salom to Sam. It was more American, they said.

Then began such a whirl of parties and events as I never dreamed existed anywhere. They took me to the movies and the vaudeville. They took me sight-seeing in country and city. To see how foolish I would be, they gave me silver coins to jingle in my pockets and spend experimentally. Moreover, I was wined and dined in a score of Syrian homes, each successive host, it seemed, trying to outdo all previous ones in fine food and tasty cooking. I had no idea I had so many relatives, uncles, aunts, nieces, nephews, and cousins, and within a few days I had met and knew all of them. My relatives honored me with a party and dance at the church, and for the first time I held a girl in my arms and tried to keep off her feet. Yes, for a few blissful days I was thoroughly and enthusiastically Americanized.

After living the life of Riley for a couple of weeks, I felt I ought to be finding work and getting out on my own. Besides, it had cost my brothers about a thousand dollars getting me here; I ought to be paying that back. So presently I got a job in the packing plant where my brother was some kind of a boss. I was put in the hide cellar, beating salt out of cured hides and repiling them or lugging them to a platform for loading into a freight car. That was the worst job I ever had. Perhaps it was only because I was soft and too small and weak for the job; perhaps because I was such an uneven match for the man I was teamed with, a big-framed, muscular giant of a fellow who chewed tobacco or snuff incessantly and spat to see how close he could shave me. We would trudge over six or seven inches of rough salt packed on the floor, climb a stack of hides cured in more salt, peel off the topmost hide, each grabbing one edge between his widespread hands, carry it down to a huge wooden block about two feet high, lift the hide high above our heads, and then beat it down with a loud clop against the block. These blows would dis-lodge the salt from the hide and send it flying into the air. Being so much shorter than my partner, I got most of the falling salt. It went down my neck in fine grains and pebbles and settled around my waist, caught there by my belt. There it dissolved in perspiration, rubbed my flesh raw, and irritated me maddeningly. When I loosened my belt to get rid of it, it crawled down my pants. Some of the undissolved pebbles would lodge in my boots, and I had to walk on them. Because he was so much stronger than I, my partner would sometimes jerk the hides from my tender hands, rubbing raw the skin on my fingers and knuckles.

That first night, I lay in bed too tired and tortured to sleep. My fingers were as raw and sore as boils. My feet were almost as bad. Every muscle in my body ached with a million aches.

In a few days big cracks were opening up in my skin. The biting salt worked into the raw places and ate at my flesh until I could have screamed and was ready to give up the ghost. But the ghost would not give up; I would not tell my brothers I could not stand the work.

But my brother saw me visibly wither and found work for me in another part of the plant. I liked my new job for one hour. All I had to do was to stand at a machine with a whirling knife in the pork-cutting department and, as the slabs of bacon slid by in endless procession, catch the skins shaved off by the knife and stack them on a truck in front of me. The room was filled with every sort of machine and hundreds of workers. Steam hissed and roared from a thousand valves, misting and darkening the vast room, the electric-light bulbs shining subdued like stars through a light mist.

When my first truckload of bacon rinds was ready, the straw boss came over to me and told me to pull it away. It was an incredible order. How could I pull that huge truck? Why, it would take an ox to budge it. Angered at my hesitancy, the boss seized the handles, lifted up and pulled forward. The load moved. He pulled it over to a scale and weighed it. Then he motioned for me to pull it away. I pulled up on the load as I had seen him do, but with a jerk. The truck rared back. The two wheels underneath slid forward against my heels at the same time that the heavy iron handles sprang up, jerking me unceremoniously off the floor. Afraid of hitting the ceiling, I let go and fell sprawling to the wet floor. The wheeler completed its somersault and scooted bacon skins all over the place. Laughing uproariously, the workers around me forgot to work, and the boss was madder than a hornet.

"—— —— you foreigner! Who ever sent you here? Why didn't they give you a nursing bottle? Come on now, you foreign runt, pick this up."

I didn't know that that was what he was saying, but another Syrian worker who helped me reload the truck translated for me. It sounds even worse in Syrian. I treasured up those words with a smoldering resentment, especially about this "foreigner" business. It made me shrink and quiver inside. From that moment, and for several years, I was to feel timid, insecure, and sensitive about every hint, every suggestion, every innuendo as to my origin. I had taken for granted that I belonged body and soul to America. Now I was not so sure. Every defeat, every failure—and I had many of them—only ground this feeling deeper into my spirit. In the pictures I have from that period, the sullen, frightening effects of this experience, repeated again and again, are plainly written on my face. I was just a sullen, unhappy, underdog immigrant, and even proudly posing for a picture couldn't erase that feeling from my photographs.

I guess my fellow countryman felt sorry for me. He helped reload the truck and wheel it to the elevator. He even accompanied me to a huge freezing room on the fifth floor and showed me what I was supposed to do—take two skins at a time, spread them out on large trays, and return the trays to the thousands of shelves which filled the place.

"When you get through," he said, before he left, "bring your truck back and load it again. If I'm around, I'll help you move and weigh it when you get it loaded."

Still smarting inside from being called a foreigner, I set

to work unloading the skins. Before the truck was empty
I was half frozen to death. I had come from a hot, steam-
ing room into this freezer where the temperature must
have been close to zero. My shirt, which had been saturated
with steam and perspiration, was now brittle as glass and
cold as ice to my skin. My oilcloth apron crackled like
cellophane. My feet became numb and my fingers almost
useless. My flesh shivered. My teeth rattled. Never before
in my life had I been so cold. I hurried almost carelessly
through the last strips and wheeled the empty truck to the
nearest door. I backed through, pulling the wheeler along,
and found myself in a room colder than the one where I
had been freezing. One look and I shuddered. There were
miles of pipe heavily sheathed and bearded with ice and
snow. I lost no time backing out of there. I tried another
door, and another and another. Always the same chilling,
frozen sight. The big freezer in which I had deposited my
load was surrounded with freezers. Just when I thought I
was doomed to a slow death by freezing, I found my way
out into a warmer climate. Now I was in a huge room
among a great number of bustling workers going in all
directions. I pulled my truck into an elevator. There were
three other workers, one of them with a truck like mine.
Each called out something, got off the elevator and left
me alone with the operator.

He said something to me. I shrugged my shoulders.

There was an unpleasant look on his face. He spoke louder. I shrugged my shoulders. He shouted into my ears, thinking, I guess, that I was deaf. I shrugged my shoulders and shook my head. He mimicked me with exaggeration and disgust.

The elevator stopped and picked up some more workers with trucks. The operator said something to them. They looked at me and laughed. I grinned. One of them said something, and I shrugged my shoulders. Then they all shrugged their shoulders. Then they all laughed. Why, I don't know. One of them put his fingers up to his head and made a circular motion. I understood that. It was Syrian sign language for crazy. I pointed at my detractors and made the same motion over my head. One of them saluted with a strange salute, putting his thumb to his nose and waving his fingers. I saluted him back. We all saluted. The other workers went out, one by one, and I was still riding up and down in the elevator. I practised the salute on the operator. He drew back his fist to punch me, then changed his mind.

Finally, the disgusted operator shoved me off. I found myself in the midst of a totally unfamiliar scene, and not a sign of anything that looked like my machine. I returned to the elevator and tried another floor, still dragging my truck behind me. I wandered up and down the aisles, hunting and hunting, with no luck. Then it dawned on me that I was lost—lost in a huge packing plant and unable to inquire my way about. I stopped a man who looked like a Syrian and asked him where I was. He couldn't understand me. I think he was an Italian. I stopped another Syrian-looking fellow. He couldn't understand me, either. I think he was a Greek. Yes, I was lost, lost in a bewildering confusion of men and meat and machinery—and I was a foreigner, and everybody else was a foreigner; we couldn't even talk to each other.

In the midst of my bewilderment I could not help but be amazed at the endless flow of miracles performed on every hand under my very eyes. Time and again, forgetting that I was lost and that somebody might be cussing the living daylights out of me, I stopped to watch some fascinating operation. I saw scores of squealing, screaming animals reduced, cut by cut, slice by slice, to the most amazing assortment of hams, cutlets, chops, and sausages. Here was the inside of the America I had seen from the outside when I sped westward on that train. Here was the intricate symphony of men and machines my schoolmaster had told me made America the industrial leader and the big brother of the whole world. I marveled at the ingenuity of the men who had conceived and built all this. They must have the powers of angels, I thought. Yes, and of devils, too, for who but a devil could invent such an odor as assailed the nostrils in the tankage room, or who but a devil could organize such a screaming pandemonium of blood and death as there was in the hog kill! But it was all too marvelous and inexplicable for my small mind to comprehend. My senses were in a whirl and my feeling of lostness, of foreignness, all the greater for the sights I stopped to see. This America was too big for me, too overwhelming. Everything was on the biggest scale in the world; even the smells, noises, and confusion were colossal.

Presently a whistle blew. I had just emerged with my truck from another elevator. Workers were dropping their tools and leaving the room, some laughing, shouting, talking, others silent, morose, or dead-pan. I just stood there wondering what to do, scanning the passing faces, unable to recognize a single soul. Suddenly the lights went out. The huge room was plunged into total darkness. What was this? I was afraid to move for fear of running or falling into something, what with all those knives and vats and awful machines around. I stepped back, got hold of my truck and sat down, hardly able to understand my predicament.

As I sat there on the truck, plenty worried about how I was going to get out of this dark room without drowning in a vat, falling into a nest of sharp tools, or maybe getting lost again in a maze of cold rooms, I became aware of something alive in the room. My flesh crept and chilled as I realized that I was surrounded with rats. They seemed to be invading the room in droves. I could see pairs of tiny pinpoints in the dark flash on and off, on and off, as they wheeled and turned. I could hear the skitter of feet on the floor, and scratching and gnawing. I could hear shrill squeals. I could hear bones crackle and meat fall to the floor. Filled with horror, I pulled my feet up on the truck and said "Whoosh!" There was a noise of a thousand feet and innumerable thuds as furry bodies hit the floor. My blood ran cold. I covered my head and screamed. I knew then I shouldn't have said "Whoosh!" They were all coming right for me. Any second a thousand bodies would smother my face in crawling fur, a thousand fangs would sink into my flesh, reduce me to a squirming mass of tattered meat. Oh, why hadn't I had sense enough to stay in Syria? Why didn't I know when I was well off? My whole past life flashed by in a moment of time. But nothing happened. The rats were gone.

While I was worrying again about how to get out of this place, the rats came back and resumed their feasting. I sat huddled and shivering on the truck, agonized over my plight. Presently the lights came back on. Then I saw them; thousands of them? No. Maybe twenty-five. Maybe fifty. My imagination had done the rest. Rats were a perennial problem around a packing plant, I was told later. But they were pretty well under control and in most departments entirely exterminated. I tried to believe that.

After more wandering about, I spotted my brother on another floor.

"What are you doing up here?" he asked.

"I'm looking for my job."

"What! Have you lost your job again?" he exclaimed.

"No, but I'm going to—I think."

And I did. But I didn't mind so very much. I had been on an unconducted tour of virtually the whole packing plant. With an empty truck as a pass, I had gone unchallenged from department to department; I had seen the miracle and ingenuity that is America. And, anyway, that was the worst job I ever had.

After a few days my brother managed to manipulate me into the hog kill. He said you couldn't get lost there. But there are many different ways of being lost. This time my job was to untangle the greasy hooks and chains which carried the hog carcasses to the dressing room. The chains were dropped through a slot in the ceiling from the department above. With a deafening clamor they hit the steel table over which I presided, whereupon I seized them in my raw, sore hands, disentangled them, and hooked them to a continuous conveyor chain which carried them to the other end of the room. There a huge, powerful-muscled Negro cornered a hog in a small pen, hooked him by a hoof, and lifted him by means of a wheel slowly into the air and switched him to a moving train overhead which took the squealing beast to his doom.

I forget how many stages of descent there are in Dante's *Inferno*, but I know there aren't as many as there are in a packing plant. Of all the places I had ever worked in, this was really the worst. Hours on end I stood above the loathsome scene listening to the incessant screaming of hogs and the ear-splitting clang of iron chains. All day long, doing the same monotonous thing, hearing the same awful noises, seeing the same hellish sight, smelling the same repulsive odor of death mingled with the suffocating odor of steam escaping from the dehairing room.

I actually wondered if this was America, the America I had dreamed so much about, the land I was ready to give my soul to come to. Cast off into space, standing above this wild, mad din, in the center of this dungeon of death, this sour, sickening odor of dirty pigs and dead blood, removed from all human company as if rotting in a cell—I wondered how I was going to learn English here, how I was going to find out what it means to be an American. My mind went back to those far-off days in Syria. I tried to remember the worst, most miserable work I had ever done there—working in the fields under a scorching sun, pulling thistles and thorns which sank into my flesh, worked up under my fingernails, and festered painfully in the quick. How I longed to be back in Syria even for just a day! At least there it was quiet, and there was sunshine and clean air and the great blue sky overhead.

It was the next day that I exploded—and then it wasn't because of the misery of my work. When I arrived at the plant that morning, the hog kill was closed. At first I thought I had come too early. Then, as the morning wore on and nobody came, I wondered what was wrong. In a way, I was glad not to have to go back into that sour, screaming room. But I wondered, too, if I was getting paid, or had I been fired, or what. I decided to look up my brother. When he saw me, he said, "What's the matter, Sam? No work today?"

"There's nobody there," I said. "What's happened?"

"Some days, Sam, they have too small a shipment of hogs to operate the department, so they shut down."

So that was it. This was the first day's work I had lost.

"How can I ever pay back what I owe you if I can't work steady?" I asked my brother indignantly.

"Oh, you'll make it back some other day. How long did you work yesterday—nine hours, wasn't it? You got one hour overtime. Some days you work short, some days long. It all evens up in the long run."

I wasn't convinced. "It isn't fair," I said. "I'm working

for this packing house. If they want me only when they need me, maybe I'll find work somewhere else. Why can't they give me other work to do?"

"They don't run things that way. Each man has his own job to do."

"When I worked in Syria, my boss kept me all the year round. One day I worked in the fields, another day I worked in the vineyard, another day I took care of the animals, but I never lost one day of work. Why, even when the weather was bad so you couldn't work, I wasn't turned out."

"Things are different here, Sam. You don't work by the year in this plant. You work by the hour."

"By the hour? Do *you* work by the hour?"

"No, my job is different, but most of the workers here work by the hour."

Then my feelings got the better of me. A look of amazement came over my brother's face as the pent-up anger and indignation that had been brewing inside of me for days poured out.

"Why didn't you tell me this before I came to America? Maybe I wouldn't have come. Syria is better than this uncertainty and killing labor. Do you live and eat by the hour? Can you build your house by the hour? Do you marry and raise children by the hour? Then why do they make men work by the hour? How can anybody know from one day to the next whether he is going to be able to eat or not? Yes, and why didn't you tell me I would have to work in a dark, wet, ugly, smelly butchering place, push trucks around like a donkey, freeze one minute and smother the next, break my back and tear my hands to pieces just to earn a bare living—and then have people tell me that I don't belong here, that I am a dumb foreigner and should go back where I came from?"

Suddenly I felt sorry I had spoken that way. My brother didn't say anything, but just stared at me in a funny, sympathetic sort of way.

"I'm sorry," I said.

"It's all right, Sam, I know how you feel."

If there is something worse than going from the sublime to the ridiculous, I went to it. My next job was to sit on a stool all day and open and shut a door over and over again to allow men riding on little trucks loaded with meat to pass in and out of a big cooling room. Of course I did not know at first that it was a cooling room. I had a growing suspicion my employers had invented this job because they felt sorry for me. I saw other doors in the plant which were closed with a heavy piece of iron or a bag of sand. So that is what they make of you when you are too useless for anything else—an animated sandbag on a pay roll, an expensive substitute for a piece of iron. The longer you stay on a job like that, the sillier you feel, and the more useless. You wonder what your friends in Syria would think if they saw you sitting here all day long on this stool, just operating a door. Open and shut, open and shut, all day long—just opening and shutting a door. Every day that job mocked me more. Contrary to my brother's promise, I had worked myself down instead of up. Beginning virtually at the bottom, I had worked myself down from department to department until now I was just a human door spring required neither to think nor learn anything new the rest of my life. There was only one consolation: I was sure I couldn't go any lower.

I wanted to talk to somebody about this door business, but I didn't bother my brother with any more complaints. So I looked up a Syrian-American one night, a man with a college education, whom I greatly admired. I told him about my silly occupation.

"Why should you complain?" he said. "You've got a soft snap, and you're getting paid good money for it, aren't you? How much do you get paid an hour?"

"I don't know. I'm not complaining about the pay, but about not really earning it."

"I don't see why you should worry about that," he said. "That's their worry. A job is a job. As long as you get your pay check, why worry about whether you earn it or not?"

"But I just sit on a box and do nothing."

"You're lucky. That's better than sweating and bleeding for your money. Besides, that's all the big bosses do. They sit on their hind ends all day and make more money than ten hard-working men put together. The head of the company parks his feet on a desk and makes millions. All you have to do, if you're smart, is to sit on that box and use your head. You can sit your way from one soft snap to another right up to the top. Use your head, Sam, use your head."

In spite of his advice I went on just using my seat. I felt deeply discontented with myself. I was a misfit in America. The useful jobs were too hard to handle, the useless jobs irked my spirit and made me feel so useless and unnecessary. Where did I belong, how could I fit into this great country? Or could I fit? That was the dreadful question: could I fit?

After weeks of tending the door and growing more sullen all the time, I had a feeling that my mind was dying within me. My ambition languished, my hope faded, my job was getting the better of me. Every day it spoke the same silent message of despair and boredom into my ears: "You aren't any good, you don't fit, you don't belong here, your home's in Syria."

Then, one day, I got mad. One of the men on a truck called me a "foreigner." From bitter experience I had learned to recognize that, to me, hateful English word. It wasn't just what he said—for I didn't fully understand him —but the way he said it that made me see red. I slammed the door on his vehicle midway between rooms, and meat went flying in all directions. I wasn't fired: I quit. I just didn't go back to that job. It was the first useful and independent thing I had done in weeks. I had asserted myself and I was free. Also I was out of a job.

CHAPTER X

Ambition to Learn English

MY NEXT JOB was in a Greek hat shop on one of the prosperous side streets of Sioux City. I took it because it looked like a much better place than the packing house to meet real Americans and learn the English language. But it didn't work. Most of my time was given to cleaning and blocking hats. The only time I met an American customer was when he didn't like the job.

In the meantime I was getting acquainted with another phase of American life my Syrian schoolmaster had forgotten to tell me about. One evening a young Syrian-American friend said to me, "C'mon, Sam, go out with us tonight. The gang's going to make whoopee. We'll get you a blind date and show you a real American good time."

Thrilled at the prospect of a real American good time, I dressed in my very best imitation of a movie sheik, Hollywood style: "sheik" was one of the few words I felt at home with in the English language because it is Arabic—although an Arabian sheik would never recognize an American one. Around nine o'clock that night a noisy horn blew outside. I dashed out to meet a Model T filled with arms and legs, boisterous laughter, and noisy chatter.

"Hiya, Sam," somebody shouted out of the general din. "Climb in the back seat."

I was no sooner squeezed in than my "blind date" began to chatter like a pneumatic hammer and blow clouds of cigarette smoke into my eyes. That was part of the good time, I guess.

Presently one of the boys said, "Sam, let's chip in and buy a pint."

"Buy who?"

"Buy a pint, get some white mule, hooch, moonshine— you know, something to drink."

"But hello, we have a law. If we drink, we break the law. The police——"

"Aw, c'mon, Sam, don't be afraid of the flatfoots. They ain't goin' to catch us. They get tanked up, too."

"But aren't you boys too proud—too ashamed, I mean— to break the law?"

"Heck, no. Everybody does it. Why, you ought to see the old grandpas cutting up down at the speakeasy."

"You're kidding me. You don't mean it."

"Heck, yes, Sam. Whasamatter with ya? C'mon, be Americanized. You don't want to be a sissy, do ya?"

I didn't want to be a sissy, whatever that was—and I knew from the scorn in their voices that it was something very terrible and un-American. Also, I knew from the way they urged me to be a good sport that that was something very wonderful. So I chipped in for a pint, and we guzzled. Then I was no longer a sissy or a poor sport. I *was* an American, a real American—and very proud of it. I told everybody we met about what a good American I was. I told them all that I wasn't one of them darn furriners.

For a while everything was changed. When you wanted to go one way, you staggered the other. Out on the highway, you saw the road twice, spinning and twisting like an injured snake. You couldn't understand how those kids could drive the same Model T on two highways; sometimes they drove on the road that wasn't there.

"C'mon, Abe," one of the party said, slobbering his words as we pushed the car out of a ditch, "get the car back on the road. You can't get the road back to the car." He must have been slightly sober, anyhow.

At a roadhouse way out in the country we "spiked" some more drinks and drank to the point of forgetting. Then everybody had an impulse to dance. They put a nickel in a music machine; the music went round and round. They put their frames together and struggled mightily to the tune of "Oh gee, Oh gosh, I can't give you anything but loooovvve, baby," or something like that.

Early in the morning we wavered home, still having a real American good time, everybody singing crazily, "Oh gee, Oh gosh, I can't give you anything but loooovvvve, babeeeeeeeee."

The whole world was worse the next morning; I didn't feel like going to work. I was sick, very sick, and the more I thought of the night before the worse I felt. What bothered me was that I had let myself fall into the same class with the drunkards, dope addicts, and degenerates whose fate my friend Abdo in Beirut had taught me to fear and despise. What bothered me about those young people I had been out with was that they were born Americans, heirs to the most precious material and spiritual heritage on earth. Within their reach were all the splendid things my Syrian schoolmaster had described to me—schools, colleges, libraries, museums, churches, cathedrals, parks, recreation centers, theaters, athletic fields. Unlike the foreigners in the packing plant, they knew the language, were educated in the American schools; in every way they were in a better position than I to take advantage of these wonderful things. Yet they passed them all up for a wild night in an illegal drinking saloon.

In my spare time I had been reading a Syrian-language book on American history and how to become a citizen. There were many things not clear to me, and I welcomed every chance to start a discussion on them. One day in a speakeasy booth (to be a good sport I still went out with the gang) I asked this out-of-place question: "What form of government is the American government?"

Said young citizen Number 1, puzzled, as if he knew the answer but couldn't think of it just then: "What form? . . . Form? Form!"—snapping his fingers and repeating, "Form . . . form . . . form," to keep the others from getting their answers in. "Oh yes, we have the best form of government there is."

Said citizen Number 2, "Oh yeah! But he don't mean that, you dope. He means what *kind* of government."

Young citizen Number 3, a girl with artificial cheeks and lips, spoke up: "Well, it ain't no Democratic government, 'cause Coolidge is president and he's Republican."

"Yah, that's it," several shouted. "It's Republican. Yay bo!"

"Well, let's see," one of them said more thoughtfully, hoping to clear things up for me, "sometimes we have a Democratic government, sometimes Republican. All depends on who's president."

A few nights later some of my friends took me to a settlement house; I think they were getting worried about my morals. Anyway, one of the social workers cornered me and with the help of a Syrian-American friend got me to tell my story. She was a very friendly, gracious person. During the whole stumbling recital she kept exclaiming, "How wonderful!" or "How thrilling!" She asked me to come back again the next night; said a friend of hers would like to meet me.

The friend was a newspaper reporter. He asked me more questions and made notes on a pad. Next day the picture of a very "immigrantish"-looking fellow appeared in the evening paper with a story that went like this:

Pursuing an ideal set up several years ago when he was a student in the antiquated school systems of Syria, Samuel Rizk now is striving to become an American citizen.

While most American boys may aspire to become a president of his country, a big-league home-run king, or a master of high finance, Samuel will be content to become an educated American, capable of serving his new homeland to the fullest degree. . . . His ambition now, as he declares it, is "to become a life servant of the United States."

When my brother translated that for me, it seemed the most beautiful idea I had ever heard—a life servant of the United States—but I couldn't for the life of me remember having declared it. That newspaperman had a wonderful imagination. And I'm glad he did. His article aroused my spirit from the hapless stupor to which my lack of progress that first year in America had brought me. It inspired me with an overpowering passion to struggle free from the discouraging milieu which made my most urgent ambitions impossible. From now on, if determination counted for anything, I was going to have a more active part in my own destiny.

I began to see my trouble and to search for means to remedy it.

In the first place, I wasn't learning the language. To spare me embarrassment as well as to expedite conversation between us, my Syrian friends were speaking to me in my own tongue. In the packing plant it was no better, for most of the workers around me were foreigners like myself. When they talked to each other they used their own language; when they talked to me they used profanity.

In the second place, I was afraid of Americans. Something in their attitude held me off, made me feel that I was something less than they were. It sometimes made me wonder if I really wanted to meet them or have them as friends. Yet when people like the social worker and the newspaper reporter befriended me, I had a feeling of being on the verge of a great discovery—the discovery of that magic land whose inner spirit my schoolmaster had described so often and so vividly.

But the other thought kept coming back over and over again, like steady dripping of rain from the eaves: "You can't be an American without English. You can't be an American without English."

That is really a dreadful feeling. You have America all around you; your feet are on her soil; your ears are filled with the music of her voice; your eyes behold the magnificence and beauty of her material achievements; yet the real America, the America you grasp with the understanding, is always eluding you because you do not have the key.

Desperate and determined, I talked it over with several friends. One of them said, "Sam, why don't you try peddling? Get out of town. Get away from the people you know. Go out to the small towns around here where there aren't any Syrians and sell oriental rugs to the Americans. Then you'll have to learn English."

It sounded like a good idea. Within a few days I had acquired a partner, Joe Solomon by name, who was working his way through school. We arranged for a consignment of rugs and tapestries and bought an old Model-T Ford. It had droopy fenders and doors that refused to stay shut. It was so tentatively hung together that every time something stopped rattling we went back and picked it up. In this seventy-five dollars' worth of mechanical trouble we set out for the hills and prairies of Iowa, Joe to earn next year's college tuition, I to learn English from American housewives in the little country towns.

CHAPTER XI

Peddler of Rugs and Tapestries

IT WAS A BEAUTIFUL SPRING MORNING the day Joe and I set out, he to make his tuition and I to learn English, and my joy in being a citizen of this bright land was almost unbounded. Everywhere, on both sides of the road as far as the eye could see, were the great farms with their big white houses, their bursting cribs and granaries, and their huge red barns—cow castles, I called them—and all the animals that belonged to the farms: cows, horses, sheep, pigs, chickens; the same unbelievable signs of prosperity and well-being which made my first days in America such an overwhelming experience. When I remarked to Joe about the richness of the countryside and the prosperous look of the farms, he said there was only one thing they needed to be complete: a lovely oriental tapestry on the living-room wall and an oriental rug on the floor.

That first day out we didn't make a single canvass. We

had five flat tires and spent almost all our time patching tubes and wrestling with stubborn rims. Between flats, Joe instructed me in the mysteries of selling and taught me to parrot stock phrases in the lore of the tapestry salesman.

The second day, having landed early in the morning in a likely-looking town, we each draped several richly colored rugs and tapestries over an arm and, taking opposite sides of the street, began knocking on doors. Across the way Joe disappeared into a home. My luck was not so good. I worked three blocks without making a single canvass. Suspicious women peeked through narrow cracks of doors, eyed me coldly, shook their heads, spoke in crisp voices, and left me standing on the porch puzzled and wondering.

After canvassing several blocks without the pleasure of even a whiff of good American breakfast, I crossed the street. A car pulled in front of me, and a red-faced farmer peered curiously at my display. "Oh boy, a sale," I thought as he came to a halt directly in my path.

"Whataya got there, buddy?"

"Rugs—oriental rugs."

"What ya doin' with 'em?"

"Sellin' 'em."

He eyed me strangely. "Had any luck?"

"Not yet."

"How long ya been here?"

"Just today."

"Have ya gotcher license?"

"Lice? No, no lice."

"A license. A license. Don't act so ignorant. You know what I mean. Where's your license?"

"No got."

"Well, yer under arrest," he said gruffly, opening the door of his flivver.

"I'm arrest? What you mean?"

"Git in. Yer goin' to jail."

"Jail?"

"That's right, jail. C'mon now, hurry it up."

"You're kiddin' me."

"No, I'm not kiddin' you. Yer under arrest. Git in."

"Who are you?"

"I'm the mayor o' this town."

I laughed. Now I knew he was kidding me. One of the things that had puzzled me about Americans was their habit of kidding. In the packing plant, at the hat shop, at church doings, at home, my friends had endless amusement at my expense because of my credulity and ignorance of modern civilization. The practical jokes they played on me would almost fill a volume. At first my response had been anger and resentment; then, as I caught on, I returned tit for tat. Now here was a man dressed in patched overalls. There was a distinct barnyard odor about him, and his battered old hat, rough hands, and red face advertised him as anything but the highest official of this town. So I said, "If you mayor, then I President," laughed, and made to walk around his car.

"Hold on there," he shouted. "Do you know the penalty for resisting an officer of the law?"

"Who?"

"You heard me." Yes, I heard him, but I didn't understand him, so I said, "I no much speak English."

"Listen, you dad-blasted furriner. Don't try to pull that'n on me. I'm onto your tricks. Every time you furriners git in a scrape with the law, you can't speak English. That ain't no alibi with me. Are you gonna git in this car or ain't you?" His red face was getting redder. He looked very sincere. I swallowed a lump in my throat.

"I'm no furriner. I'm American."

"You ain't no Yankee American."

"I'm American."

"If you're American, this ain't the United States. C'mon, git in this car before . . ." He went on talking half under his breath and, as I was too bewildered to move, he seized my rugs, tossed them into the back seat, then pushed me into the front. If this farmer was kidding me, he was carrying the joke a long way.

He actually did put me in jail.

I had been sitting there in the cell about three hours, contemplating my fate and wondering about Joe, when a key grated in the iron door and there was the mayor, with Joe behind him. I started to say something, but the words died on my lips. Joe screwed up his face violently and clapped his hand over his mouth. We talked in Syrian. First thing Joe said was, "Pretend not to know me."

"Why?"

"He doesn't know I'm selling, too."

"Why, is it a crime to sell?"

"It is in this town, I guess—if you don't have a license. Have you sold anything yet?"

"No."

"Well, I'll have to pay your fine, then. But you have to wait here till I sell some more rugs."

Joe left. Late in the afternoon he returned, paid the fine, and I was free again. As we rattled out of town in our decrepit machine, I said to Joe, "Why didn't you tell me mayors don't wear uniforms? I thought he was kidding me."

"Ha, ha, ha, ha! You insulted him. Ha, ha, ha, ha!" Joe almost collapsed from merriment.

"Sure, I insulted him. But he looks like a bum."

"You don't really expect a mayor to be dressed in uniform, do you?" Joe asked incredulously.

"Well, good clothes, anyway. He's an official, isn't he? But I still think he's a bum."

"Even bums can be elected mayors in this country if they can get enough votes."

Something else had been troubling me, too. "Joe," I asked, "why does everybody call me a foreigner?"

Joe pushed his hand under his hat and scratched his head reflectively.

"Because you look like one, I guess. You talk and act like one."

"But I'm not a foreigner. I'm just as much an American as people who were born here."

"Yes, but they don't know that. They just go by appearances. You don't look or act any different from millions of other immigrants in this country, and you can't expect to be treated any better than they are. What do you say we go to Minnesota?"

One place is as good as the next when everywhere is the same, so I said it was O.K. with me. I was ruminating Joe's words about my being just like all the other foreigners. It sounded as final as fate, predetermined, unalterable. I fell into a glum reverie of remorse, almost blaming myself for not being born in my own country. Why did I have to be born in Syria, anyway, and fall heir to all this contempt, ridicule, and abuse? Why should anybody have to suffer for the accident of being born in the wrong country? Besides, what was wrong with being a foreigner? Weren't all Americans foreigners if you only went back far enough? I was rebellious—and worried. Suppose the American housewives didn't like my accent or my dark face. I didn't tell Joe, but it would have suited me if he'd turned around and headed back for Sioux City.

Three days later two Syrian peddlers were selling rugs and tapestries on the elm-shaded streets of Albert Lea—with a license. For some unexplainable reason Joe's luck soured, and now I was getting into the homes and making the sales. At the end of the first day we tallied results: Salom, $108; Joe, 000. I felt pretty good.

We rambled around Minnesota and northern Iowa the rest of the summer, striking it lucky here, not so lucky there. One town was a regular bonanza. I never saw people so crazy for oriental things. Before we left we had nicknamed it Little Arabia.

On the financial side that summer was a fair success. On the grammatical side it was a flop. My English was, if anything, more atrocious than ever. It was a polyglot mixture of packing-house profanity, Syrianized slang, hat-shop lingo, and hybrid sales chatter. In a desperate effort to shed the profanity I took to substituting the word "Hello." It was an omnibus expression providing emotional outlet for every type of explosion or distress. If something puzzled me it was "Hello?" If something went wrong it was "Hello!" If something went terribly wrong it was a shouted, angry "Hello!! Hello!!!" The most descriptive, overworked adjective in my vocabulary was "lousy." It was the universal word to describe all the extremes of good, bad, or indifferent, size, height, weight, shape, color, quality, and quantity. Before the summer was over, everything was "lousy," including the English language—the way I spoke it.

The last of August we drove through a beautiful gold-and-green patchwork of harvested hills and prairies, tall corn and fluffy groves, and landed in the neat little city of Ames, Iowa. Joe wanted to continue his studies in the college there, and I was to return to Sioux City with the unsold goods and what was left of the Model T. I looked forward to this homeward trip with great anticipation. It would mark my first journey in a car alone—pride, freedom, maturity.

But I never got back to Sioux City—not that time. When our rattletrap rolled down Lincoln Way past the college campus, my eyes almost popped.

"That's the school," Joe said matter-of-factly.

School? Why, it was my dream school, the kind of place with great green lawns, crystal lakes, graceful trees, and spacious buildings that my old schoolmaster had told me about. For the first time in America I beheld the spot which struck the same chord as had Elias Khoury. It was almost as if I could see his face and his lips moving between me and this peaceful, soothing scene, picturing it into existence. We drove over the cool winding roads that rambled through the trees and around the campus. That's

Lake LaVerne, Joe said, that's the library, and that's this and that's that.

I was in raptures. "This is where you go to school, Joe?"

"Yes sir, and it's one of the best schools in the country."

"Joe," I said, "I'm going to stay here. I'm going to school here."

"You can't do that!" Joe exploded. "You can't do this to me. Who's going to take the Ford back, who's going to return the tapestries?"

"I don't know. Send them back on the train. I'm staying here."

Joe couldn't budge me. None of his arguments was any good; so he gave up and said, "Well, we can junk the car. It's got one wheel in the junk yard, anyhow. But we'll have to sell the tapestries."

Gladly I'd do anything, sell a carload of tapestries, if I could only cinch this chance to get into that school. One thing bothered me: I didn't have very much money. Joe encouraged me on that score: he was catching my enthusiasm. "Sam," he said, "don't let a little thing like that worry you. In America you can work your way through school. Thousands of us do it, and you can do it too."

The next day I set out to get rid of the rest of our oriental art. I was having indifferent success when I knocked on Jim Wilson's door. He was a slender, wiry man of medium height, rusty hair and complexion, with the beginnings of a very fetching perpetual grin in the corners of his mouth. He seemed very much interested in my stuff. He fingered the tapestries, critically dug into the rug pile, shook his head. "You say that's handmade?"

"Yes sir."

"I'm sorry," he said, "but it isn't. These pieces were made on a machine."

"Hello!" I said, feeling surprised and embarrassed. "But they told me this is handmade."

"No, it isn't. Come on in and I'll show you some real rugs."

Inside, he pointed to a huge hanging carpet of strange design. "What do you think of that?" he asked proudly.

"Beautiful!" I said. "Where did you get it?"

"Africa."

"Africa?" I had stirrings of vague memories—fag-end recollections of stories Abdo had told me.

"Yes," Jim said, the grin spreading over his whole face, "I took a crazy trip through Africa a couple of years ago. Went on a motorcycle and darn near didn't come back. When my side kick and I left Cairo, the British officers were betting twenty to one we'd never make it."

I felt a great deal in common with this man and strangely attracted to him. He had been in my part of the world. Yes, he knew more about it than I did, a lot more.

We talked for some time, Jim patiently, humorously explaining things in words I could understand. You could tell he was used to talking to people who didn't know his language. He told me how he and his buddy "three-wheeled" through Africa with motorcycle and sidecar and exploded the popular myth of a blood-and-thunder land where fierce cannibals craved white man's meat and dangerous animals were forever on the prowl. He had found the naked savages friendly, fascinating, and enjoyable. He had lived with them, eaten their food African style, dabbled in their arts, danced their dances, and trotted their babies on his knees. With an old banjo he had taken American jazz to the jungle and made such an impression that an admiring chieftain offered him a bribe of half a dozen wives to stay. The rugs, pottery, and drums in this room, Jim said, were trophies of his trip. He hadn't decided yet just what he wanted to do with them.

Then a charming young woman came in, and Jim introduced her as his wife. I could understand then why he turned down a whole harem of African beauties to come back to the United States.

Before I left he invited me back and warned me again about machine-made goods. I didn't know it then, but meeting Jim Wilson was one of the biggest breaks of my life. His inspiring friendship and example were to prove a strong factor in some of my later plans.

CHAPTER XII

Struggles with English

Now that i was determined to go to school in Ames, I must find some other kind of work. One thing I knew I could not do: I could not go on peddling rugs and tapestries —not after my meeting with Jim Wilson. Something inside me would keep saying (I was still doing most of my think· ing in Syrian), "*Gashash, gashash, gashash* [You're a fake, you're a fake, you're a fake]," and my tongue would be tied and I would not be able to muster enough courage even to knock on a door.

It was early September, and the opening of the fall term of college was still a couple of weeks away. Joe had gotten a job waiting on tables at a café which catered to the col· lege trade. I appealed to him for help, and several days later he told me there was an opportunity at the same café for a good dishwasher if I wanted to take it. Would I be willing? Well, I got over to the café as fast as I could, and in ten minutes I was in an apron, wielding a dishcloth and clattering dishes with all that fresh enthusiasm which a new job always commands.

At the very first opportunity I set out to arrange for a college education. I inquired my way across the almost deserted college campus to the administrative offices and had a revealing interview with a very kind gentleman by the name of Foster. He was the dean of the summer school, but that didn't mean anything to me. I thought of him only as some kind of high government official in whose presence I must feel timid and respectfully awed.

"I want to go to college," I told him.

"How much work have you had, Mr. Rizk?" he asked.

"Work? Well, I work packing plant, Sioux City. Then I peddle rugs."

He smiled broadly. "I mean how much college work."

"I no work in college," I replied. "I work café now."

By that time Mr. Foster had my number, and he quizzed me along another line. Before I knew it I had told him my story, that I had been in the country not quite two years, that I couldn't speak English, and that I wanted to learn to be an American like other Americans.

"Well," Mr. Foster finally said, "what you want to do is to go down to the high school and see Mr. Davis. He's the superintendent and a very kind man. He'll be glad to help you out."

He then gave me careful directions as to how to get there and bade me good-by and good luck.

The next day I went to see Mr. Davis. Riding on the bus the two miles between West Ames, or college town as it was sometimes called, and downtown Ames, I had plenty of time to think, and I began to be worried. Mr. Foster had assured me that Mr. Davis was a kind man, and I did not doubt that. But could I make myself clear? Could I, with my limited command of the English language, make him understand how hungry I was to learn English? Then a dreadful thought came to me: maybe I was going to be pushed around and put off, the way I had been in Beirut when I went to the consulate for my passport. By the time the bus discharged me in front of the school I was worked into a painful state of nervous anxiety.

The school was a large building of well-weathered brick, without the wide expanse of well-kept lawn and winding avenues of tall trees the college had.

When I entered the building I drew from my pocket a card on which Mr. Foster had printed Mr. Davis' name in large letters. As I walked down the hall, I examined the name plates on the doors and compared them with the printing on the paper. When I found the matching name, I walked into the office and was asked by a gentleman what I wanted.

"I want to go to school to learn English," I said.

The interview was brief and just as I had feared. Mr. Davis said something about "elementary" and used other big words. He asked me where I came from and what schooling I had.

"I'm sorry," he said shortly, "but you do not know enough English to enter high school. There is nothing we can do for you."

Something seemed to fall hard inside of me, to go out of me, and a big lump came up in my throat. I mumbled "Thank you," finding my voice with difficulty, and stumbled into the hall. Blinding tears were fighting their way out of the corners of my eyes. I walked without knowing just where. I did not know English, and I could not learn English until I knew English! I was caught in a vicious circle and could not work or fight my way out.

I stopped to wipe my eyes, ashamed to be seen in tears, and when I looked up I saw a big glass cupboard full of shining objects, large, glittering cups, like the silver chalices in our churches, only much bigger, and metal figures of running men with helmets on their heads and egg-shaped balls tucked under their arms. I realized that this was not the way I had come in, but I continued down the hall till I rounded a corner. There I saw another door with the name "Davis" on it. Or was it the same "Davis"? Surely I hadn't come back to the same office. Could it be, I thought after a moment, that there was another Davis? I got out the paper with Mr. Foster's printing on it. Yes, it was the same name. I walked back down the hall whence I thought I had come and looked at the first door again. Yes, it said Mr. Davis, too. There were two Mr. Davises. Maybe I had talked to the wrong one.

I was caught between two impulses, one to stay and the other to flee. I hesitated, unable to decide what to do. I walked up and down the hall, stopped several times to stare into the trophy case, gulped water at the drinking fountain, even decided to leave, and then changed my mind. Finally I felt enough nerve to try the other Davis.

A very nice-looking girl sitting at a big desk asked me if I wanted to see Mr. Davis. I said yes, I did.

"He's busy just now," she said and smiled. "Won't you sit down?"

I sat down and waited, still feeling uneasy. I hung my hat on one knee, and it fell to the floor. I bent over to pick it up, and my long hair fell over my face. Brushing it back, I suddenly became aware of my hands; I didn't know what to do with them. I crossed them on my lap and stared at them intently. They looked very rough and ungainly, and the knuckles were creased with dirt from cleaning the boss's basement that morning. I noticed that the cuffs of my shirt were soiled, that my coat sleeves were frayed, that my shoes were scuffed and unshined and very dusty, that my trousers were greasy and horribly wrinkled. I felt more unkempt and alien than when I first arrived on the boat in New York. Suddenly a panic seized me. I was almost frightened at myself, at my audacity in thinking that such a wild creature as I was could make an impression with clean, well-dressed, educated Americans. I was on the point of running away, but some sort of inertia made me sit. I began to wish the girl would go from the room. She was smiling about something—about me, I thought. I tried to find something on the ceiling to examine, then the walls and floor. Unsuccessful, I looked out of the window and tried to focus my attention on a tree, too miserable and embarrassed to think of what I might want to say.

"Mr. Davis will see you now," the girl said.

I walked self-consciously into the next room.

"I am Sam Rizk," I said. "Mr. Foster, he send me."

Mr. Davis stood up, extended his hand in greeting, and smiled so warmly that I wondered why I had been so scared.

"What can I do for you today?" he asked.

"I come from old country, Syria," I told him. "I want to learn English, to write and talk."

"That's a very worthy ambition. How old are you, Sam?"

"Twenty," I said, embarrassed. But his face never changed.

"How much schooling have you had?"

"Schooling?" I puzzled.

"Yes, how long have you gone to school?"

"In Syria, few months. In America, no."

"But you speak some English?"

"Yes, a little. I learn from other people talking."

Mr. Foster was right. Mr. Davis was a kind man. He made me feel easy; it seemed that I could speak better English already.

We talked for a long time, and then Mr. Davis said I could come back again the next day and I would be given a test to decide what grade I should be put in.

When I got up to leave, I asked, "How much I pay?"

"Pay? Nobody has to pay, Sam."

"Somebody has to pay."

"Oh." He laughed. "Yes, somebody has to pay. The taxpayer pays."

"Taxpayer?" I said, bowing. "Thank you, taxpayer."

Mr. Davis laughed again.

"But I have to buy books."

"No, Sam, the community takes care of that."

Marvel after marvel! I go to school and don't have to pay. I use books and don't have to buy them. What nice people these are—taxpayer and community! Someday I must meet them, yes I must see them and speak my gratitude for all this wonderful opportunity. So ran my thoughts as I took leave of my new schoolmaster, a very kind man, Mr. Davis.

"By the way, Sam," he said as I left, "I'd like to have you come over for a meal some evening next week and meet my family. Mrs. Davis would love to have you."

How thrilled I was! How overcome with an unspeakable feeling of gratitude! I ran out with such wild elation beating in my heart that I fell down the steps and skinned my elbow. No matter now. I was going to school. I had found a new schoolmaster as helpful and kind as my old one in Syria, the one who told me I was an American. Here was a schoolmaster who would help me to learn the language of America. Now life would settle down for me, I would find my place in this great land. I was on my way, and the world danced joyously under my feet.

It was decided to start me out in the fourth grade. Imagine how I felt, a grown man in long pants going to school with a bunch of kids, little boys in knee breeches and little girls in short frocks. When the full force of this discrepancy struck me, I knew I was not going to like school. I expected the youngsters to make fun of me, to laugh at my ignorance, my backwardness, and my awful accent. Strangely, nothing of the kind happened. Sometimes they would laugh at the way I scrambled the language, but it was not in ridicule. It was all in good hearty fun which I enjoyed as much as they did.

Both my teachers and my little classmates were exceedingly helpful. My eagerness to learn the English language was equaled by the enthusiasm of my teachers to help me. I was like a child learning his first words, and they almost applauded me every time I acquired a new word or turned a new sentence. My progress seemed to give them endless pleasure, and this spurred me on to extra effort.

By applying myself in my spare time and through special tutoring from my teachers I was able to move ahead rapidly. Every few weeks came a promotion until, by the end of the semester, I was ready for ninth-grade English.

I hadn't worked long on the English language, however, before I was convinced I could not depend on logic to learn it. I thought at first it would be something like my native tongue, that if you learned the letters of the alphabet and their sounds, plus some rules of grammar and spelling, you could learn by yourself.

But I had not counted on the English language being so unreasonable. There was, for example, a whole mess of sounds which were not represented in the alphabet. So it seemed somebody had gone to the trouble to juggle the letters until they fell into the most astonishing combinations, *ch, sh, ph, gh* being only among the least unpronounceable cases. After struggling for hours with certain alphabetical monstrosities, I was convinced that no one without English ancestors could ever hope to discover their sounds. But even worse than all this, when there was a very obvious letter in the alphabet to stand for a sound, somebody had labored to invent combinations which defied all my attempts at pronunciation. It was my habit to hunt in the dictionary for new words to add to my vocabulary, and one day I came across a real freak: "phthisic." How do you pronounce that? *Phth?* I find there is a simple letter in the alphabet to stand for the sound this four-letter behemoth is supposed to make. It is the letter *t*, twenty letters down in the alphabet and not so hard to find, either. Yet here is this *phth*, a monument to Anglo-Saxon ingenuity—one sound, four letters, and you have to guess which one to pronounce. I used to puzzle no end over words like "freight" and "weight," and I don't understand yet why the word "colonel" is mispronounced so badly. Many times I would despair of either learning or reforming a language which behaved so unreasonably.

And then I had to memorize a whole chaos of vowel sounds, long *a*, short *a*, broad *a*, etc., etc., etc. The letter *a*, in fact, was the worst offender, the black sheep in the vowel family. And a close second was his fat brother, the letter *o*, with six different noises to his credit. The letter *e* with a little less criminal talent has only five, yet it could be at times as wicked as the worst. But the letter *i*—I have a special affection for the letter *i*. It comes the nearest to being a second cousin of the Syrian vowels of any letter in the English alphabet. It has only two sounds and does not require you to take singing lessons before you can hit them.

Pronouns used to give me a lot of trouble, too. i would puzzle over them a whole evening. They behaved with no more respect for law and order than the vowels or those distressing consonant combinations. It seemed to me that if it is right to say "he," "his," "him," why shouldn't it follow: "she," "shis," "shim"? But no. The pundits had to make it "she," "her," and "hers" and complicate the whole business of the immigrant trying to become a good American.

All these peculiarities made it infinitely harder for me to learn the language, and sometimes I was indignant with the anonymous fathers of a tongue which I could not learn by myself. I had to wait for my teacher or some friend to help me pronounce almost every single word.

I asked one of my teachers about all this.

"Are there no rules to the English language?"

"Yes, most certainly, there are rules," she assured me "but there are exceptions to the rules."

But that did not seem to explain the difficulty. Later the real explanation came out: there were not only exceptions to the rules, but exceptions to the exceptions.

I was particularly bothered by the exceptions to the forming of plurals. I was told that the plural of any word was made by adding s or es, but when I made "foot" into "foots," I learned that was wrong. It was "feet," just as the plural of "tooth" is "teeth." Well, I had discovered a new rule. But when I made the word "booth" into "beeth," my teachers said the old rule applied and it was "booths." By this time my mind was so full of confusion that I was almost in a mood to stick to my native Syrian.

I went on to learn to my astonishment that "mouse" does not become "mouses" the way "house" becomes "houses" and that it is never right to say "hice" for the plural of "house" the way you say "mice" for the plural of "mouse" or "lice" for the plural of "louse." But how was I supposed to tell? The plural of "sheep" is neither "sheeps" nor "shoop," but "sheep," just like the singular, right straight through to ten million or even a billion billion of them. But a "baby beef" in the herd is not "baby beef" or "baby beefs" or "baby boofs," but "baby beeves." They told me that "ox" does not become "oxes" as "box" becomes "boxes." Then, when I thought I had found a clue, namely, that live things form different plurals from inanimate things, and proceeded to make "foxen" out of "fox," the teachers told me I was wrong again. They said it was "foxes." What was I to do? I was ready to appeal to the legislature for a law and make it just plain "oxen" and "foxen" and "boxen."

At last there was nothing for me to do but to memorize all this and get used to it. But sometimes I revolted, especially when my ignorance of how to spell or pronounce the language brought me embarrassment.

One day I was ordering a meal in a restaurant. It was

just before the repeal of prohibition. On the menu they had "spiced tomato juice." I had just learned that the letter *c* is sometimes pronounced hard, as in "cat." So after studying for a while I ordered "spiked tomato juice" and was icily informed that they did not serve liquor there.

During this first year in school came one of my greatest astonishments: that Americans—especially young school-going Americans—took their many blessings and opportunities so much for granted. That everybody could speak and write and worship as he pleased did not seem strange to anybody. That education was free for everyone down to the humblest of citizens amazed no one. In Ain Arab I used to long for just one sheet of paper to write on. I hungered for just one book to read, one book to call my own, and I used to rescue scraps of Syrian newspaper from the gutters of Beirut, take them home, and feast on them a whole evening. But here in America books and papers were everywhere, the schools were as magnificent as palaces and the equipment comfortable, stimulating, breath-taking. I was fascinated by all the richness, the maps and pictures on the walls, the great blackboards, all the high windows, and the many lights which were turned on when it was cloudy outdoors. How could anyone take all this grand achievement for granted?

I saw these precious privileges and opportunities wasted

by too many young Americans who evidently could not comprehend what my experience had forced upon me: the difference, the unbelievable contrast, between that old world their forefathers had left and this new world they had built. I saw youngsters actually despising the school and what it stood for, showing contempt for those who were brighter or studied harder than they did. I saw them playing hooky, pretending sickness, "getting by" with as little learning as possible. Some of them boasted of their skill in cheating and laughed up their sleeves at their un-witting teachers. They disfigured the beautiful surround-ings lavished upon them, carving their initials on the furniture and marking up the walls.

I could not understand at first how anyone could be so heedless, so negligent, and even contemptuous of these hard-won common possessions. I learned how the ances-tors of these students had worked and fought and sacri-ficed for the rights they took so much for granted. The more I dug into American history, reading much of it in the Syrian language, the greater became my astonishment. I felt that I ought to do something to awaken my fellow Americans to all these blessings. I now had a new, power-ful incentive to learn the language of the country of which I was fortunate enough to be a citizen.

Strangely, I did not recognize my first opportunity to dis-cuss appreciation of American democracy, and only gradu-

ally did it dawn upon me that I had found the avenue
which was to become a career for me. It happened this way.
One day the teacher asked the class to write a theme.

"But I cannot write," I told her.

"You can talk, though, can't you, Sam?" she said, smiling at me.

"Yes, I can talk—a little, but I can't write themes."

"Suppose that, instead of writing a theme, you tell us
your story."

"Tell my story?"

"Yes, tell us something about yourself, your life in Syria,
how you found out you were an American, your struggles
to reach this country, and how you feel about things. You
don't have to make it long, and I know it will be interesting
to all of us."

The more I thought of that assignment, the more it terrified me. I had never stood before an audience in my life.
I had told my teacher that my talk would be lousy, and I
was sure it would. I looked forward to the ordeal with the
same misgivings which torment a soldier the first time he
goes into the firing line.

Four days later I stood before nearly forty youngsters.
My knees promptly became as weak as jelly, my tongue as
heavy as a mountain, my throat dry. My hands felt as big
as those packing-house hams. After an eternity of silence,
during which I adjusted my hands and feet in all the awk-

ward positions I could think of, my tongue came free and I began to use it. The first thing I said was, "Hello!" Everybody laughed.

Twenty-five minutes later I sat down, hardly aware of the time that had passed. The youngsters were clamoring for more. But the ordeal was over. I had not imagined that anyone could forget himself so completely. Speaking and sleeping have at least one thing in common: when you get through you don't know just how long you've been at them.

Of course I was pleased by this success, even though it was only with forty school kids. But I knew it was not due to my skill with the language. It was the power of the story itself. Anybody else living through the same experience could have done as well, probably better.

Within the next few weeks I addressed nearly all the classes in the school. My teacher told the other teachers, and they invited me to repeat my story to their pupils. With each telling my confidence mounted. Each time I tried to use a wider range of words, tried to get the feel of phrases which would mean the most to the youngsters. All these opportunities to speak were a great encouragement to me and gave my tussles with the English language extra motive and determination. When the teachers began to tell me how they were awakened to a new appreciation of their American blessings, I began to see my story as the answer to this growing desire within me.

The next semester I was taking high-school English. One day the speech teacher said to me:

"Sam, wouldn't you like to take part in some extra-curricular activity?"

"Extracurricular?" I said, puzzled, wrapping my tongue around the word as best I could.

"Yes, something besides your regular English studies, something like Gymnasium, Dramatics, or Glee Club."

"What do you think I could do best?" I asked.

"Here is a list of activities. Why don't you look them over and check the one you want?"

I studied the list, wondering what it was all about, finally making a mark after "Glee Club."

"Do you know what Glee Club is?"

"No, but I'll try anything once."

"Glee Club is singing, and really, Sam, I don't think you'll make much of a singer."

"No, I'm a lousy singer. Maybe you give me something where I speak—or learn speaking better."

"Sam, why don't you try oratory? We have a high-school contest in oratory, and I think I can find an oration that will suit you just fine."

So I found out what an oration was. They gave me one to memorize entitled "The Immigrant Speaks." I didn't know the meaning of all the words, and learning to pronounce them was like memorizing nonsense. But I worked hard at it. Wherever the teacher said to lift my voice, I lifted it; wherever to lower it, I lowered it. Wherever she said to put a gesture, I put it. It was all as mechanical as operating an automobile, a push-button performance, but the teacher said it was good, especially the sincerity. Well, I was beginning to understand a little of what I was saying.

The night of the local contest I took the bus down to the school, delivered "The Immigrant Speaks" to a large audience, and returned immediately to the restaurant to scrub floors.

About ten-thirty the telephone rang.

"Hello, is this Sam Rizk?" a woman's voice asked.

"Yes, this is Sam Rizk."

"Sam, congratulations. You won."

"I one?"

"Yes, you won. Isn't that wonderful?"

"I one? Sure I one. I am not two."

"No, no, Sam. This is Mrs. Gaunt. You have first place in the speaking contest."

So I had first place! I one. This English language had a little logic to it after all. When you count, the first number is one. If you get first in a contest, you one. It was oneder-ful. Maybe I would be an American yet, a real American speaking English like other Americans.

But soon I was to suffer a blow to this slender hope. In the district oratorical contest, I lost. The judges said the oration was fine, sincere, forceful, impressive, well delivered, but alas, they said, "The Immigrant Speaks" with an accent.

CHAPTER XIII

A Dishwasher Addresses Rotary

ONE NOON AT THE RESTAURANT I was up to my elbows in dishwater when my Greek boss led a tall, pleasant-faced, neatly dressed gentleman to the kitchen.

"Mr. Rizk," the man said, "I am Mr. Forman. I happen to be president of Rotary this year, and I have been trying to build an interesting and worth-while program for the club. My daughter in high school has been telling me about you and the fine talk you gave in the auditorium several weeks ago. The Rotary Club would like to have you as their guest at luncheon two weeks from today, and they would like to have you talk to them on Americanization."

"Haven't I seen you over at the college, Mr. Forman?" I asked.

"Yes, you probably have." He smiled. "I'm in the agronomy department."

"He's the head of the department," a student whispered to me as he left.

Imagine this, a college professor, head of the agronomy department, president of the Rotary Club, a scholar, a gentleman, a prosperous citizen, going to the kitchen at the back of a restaurant to ask a poor, greasy, immigrant dishwasher to eat lunch with prominent business and professional people and to give them a talk on Americanization! I was too astonished and thrilled to think of the difficulty of the task.

When the gentleman was gone, my Greek boss started to laugh.

"This is a screwy country," he said. "The pipuls are nuts. I thought it all the time, but now I know it."

"What you mean?" I said. "These people are good."

"Yes, yes, they good. But you! You! They ask you to spik! Are you good?"

And he laughed some more and held his fat stomach under his apron.

"They have hundred professor here. They have man who have travel and write book and do big t'ing, and they want to listen to you. It is crazy, I tell you, but when pipuls do crazier things dese crazy American do dem."

"It's not crazy," I came back belligerently. "I'm going to talk to them about America, about democracy and how I like it."

And then he laughed some more, until I had to laugh, too, but sheepishly.

"T'ink, t'ink," he cried, waving his arms, "they ask you, a bum Syrian immigrant, a dishwasher in a Greek restaurant, to spik to them about de democracia. Democracia! You know where democracia come from? You know, aye? It come from Greece. If they should want to know about democracia, they should ask a Greek, not a Syrian who work in a Greek kitchen. In my country we do not listen to dishwashers. We listen to big men, philosopher, t'inker, high-class pipuls. Ha, ha, ha, ha. This very funny, very funny."

And he laughed and laughed; all the kitchen help laughed with him. I could have crawled down the kitchen drain, I felt so small. And I began to think he was right. I could think of nothing to defend myself.

"You go give talk on democracia," he started in again. "You give talk on citizenship. Then what? You get your name in paper. If he say nice t'ing about you and I like it, I promote you. That's what. I make you waitress. You bringa the coffee and the hamburg, you bringa the rosta biff from the kitchen to the pipuls on the table, and you can learn English from dem. Ha, ha, ha, ha. It make me laugh. You who cannot wait table are going to spik to Rotary Club on democracia, on American citizenship. Are you a citizen?"

"Yes," I said, making a last effort to defend myself.

"How are you citizen?"

"From being born I am a citizen."

"From being born you are a citizen," he roared. "Three years you be in America. I be here twenty-three years. I am not a citizen. No. I study to be citizen. Tomorrow I go see judge. He ask me question, hard question, see? To be a citizen I work, I study. But from being born you are a citizen. Maybe from being born you can cook. Maybe from being born you can wash dishes. Maybe from being born you can tich me how to be citizen, no? Maybe from being born you can read this book on how to be American citizen. You see dis big words. 'Cor-r-r-nstinushun—frumda-mental law of the land,' " he read from the book.

"Come, come, can you read it? 'Legislahshur-r-r-r, legis-lahtohr-r, he who makes law.' Can you answer dose question, aye? No! And you go spik to Rotary Club on American citizen! Kamato, stichraso! Ashterialo! Go to hell," he concluded scornfully and went about his business.

What could I say to my boss? He was right. I could not pronounce the big words in his book about becoming an American citizen. The word "constitution"? I could not pronounce it. "Legislature"? He could say that better than I could. I thought he had the right to laugh at me and even at those who had been foolish enough to invite me to speak to them.

As I fished halfheartedly for silverware in the dishwater, I kept turning over in my mind what my boss had said to me. And the more I thought about it, the more I knew he was right. I had really been living an ugly lie without knowing it. I had been fooling myself. When I was borne into the shining harbor of New York City, I came in like the waves of the sea, riding in the daylight, believing I saw clearly what I wanted my life to be, free from all bitterness, free from hate and pride and fear, free from all pretense and falsity. But something had happened. Perhaps like the waves I had been caught in the undertow and pulled into the murky half-light of the undersea. When my spirit fell upon prejudice on these shores, prejudice against the foreigner; when it fell upon other men's pride and fear, it was swept back, partly at least, into the darkness I had sought to escape. To defend myself against prejudice I was falling back on the fact that I was born better than other immigrants, born a foreigner, yes, but an American nevertheless. That was my pride, the thing that set me apart from and above the common run of American immigrants. Now I saw the wrongness of that. "From being born" I had no right to call myself a citizen. That was too easy, too much like having something handed to me on a platter. "From being born" people in the old country are pashas and sultans. "From being born" people in Europe are aristocrats—dukes, duchesses, and kings. But in free America mere birth bestows no privileges upon me. In America citizenship is not just something I am born with. It is something I have to earn, and I had not earned mine. I had not even earned the right to speak to an American club on this one theme which had become my driving obsession: American citizenship.

I still had two weeks before speaking at the Rotary luncheon, so I sat in my room every night till midnight poring over my English books, studying the grammar books and the spelling books, searching the dictionary for just the right words to express my meaning. I was determined to earn the right to speak, to tell my story, to be a worthy and helpful citizen of this great democracy. I began to prepare a speech on Americanization. When I was alone I walked up and down the floor, speaking aloud, telling my thoughts to the four walls until I was sick of them and began to wonder how anybody else could be interested in them.

It is hard to describe the mixture of feelings I had the day I was to speak to the Rotarians. I was thrilled and I was dismayed. One moment I felt an enormous pride, the next moment I felt a foreboding shame. First I could not make the morning hurry fast enough, and then I wished it would drag on forever. What if I failed? What if they didn't like it? What if they called it off? Just what? I wavered between an agony of doubt and an ecstasy of hope.

There was nothing else in the world for me that morning except that one event, and I was not sure I wanted to face it.

I had dressed in my best clothes, a cheap suit of black broadcloth, and shined my shoes till they gleamed like a black looking-glass. My hair, which was coarse, thick, and unruly, I soaked in a heavy bath of oil and plastered it down with a skullcap, which I wore all morning. I tried to look and feel as much like a businessman as possible. But it was not possible. The harder I tried to look like an American businessman, the more I felt like an immigrant dishwasher.

Just before noon a member of the club called for me in his car. I hastily discarded the skullcap, threw off my apron, got into my coat, adjusted my tie, wiped the dish-water from my shoes, and went out to the dining room to be greeted with a smile and a handshake so warm and strong that all my fears and doubts melted as if in the sun.

As I proudly left the café, escorted by my host and wearing my distinction like a crown, my boss pulled me back to earth with a jerk.

"Adios, Demosthenes," he yelled.

My friends—the students eating at the tables, the waiters dishing food at the counters—burst into such uproarious laughter that I had to grin myself, had to grin at my pouter-pigeon presumption.

Yes, I was not a Demosthenes. I was just a—— Then, suddenly, it came to me. I knew what I would say when I got up to speak.

"Please do not think I am a speaker," I would say. "I am not a speaker. I am a dishwasher. I am not going to make a speech. I am just going to tell you my story."

At the hotel where the meeting was held I was literally overwhelmed, almost embarrassed with kindness. The members of the club and their guests were gathered in the lobby. Everybody seemed to know me, but I did not know them. Mr. Davis, the superintendent of the schools, was there and my speech teacher, Mrs. Gaunt. They took charge of me and led me to the speakers' table. On it was a display of the flags of all the nations. I could pick some of them out—the British Jack, the French tricolor, the emblems of Italy and Turkey and Greece. I had seen them on ships passing through the Mediterranean, crossing the Atlantic, and anchored in the harbor at New York. I asked Mr. Davis about them. He said Rotary was international, a club for businessmen in all the nations, an organization standing for service and good will and peace and fair play for all, everywhere in the world.

With that everything went flat inside of me. I felt insignificant and ashamed, assailed with doubts about my appearing here. Why should I speak to these people? What could I say to them that they did not already know, that any one of them could not say better than I could? World-minded Americans, with thoughts as big as all the nations put together, and I was presumptuous enough to think they might enjoy hearing about me, my story, my feelings about their country!

But I was soon swept out of this mood by the singing of "America," everybody facing the flag and singing reverently:

> *My country 'tis of thee,*
> *Sweet land of liberty,*
> *Of thee I sing;*
>
> . . . .
>
> **Let Freedom ring.**

We had not yet finished our dessert when Mr. Forman, the president of the club, got up to make some announcements. Then he introduced the superintendent of the schools, and then the superintendent of the schools introduced my teacher, and then my teacher introduced the personnel director of the college, Dr. Helser, and just when I was thinking that everybody was going to introduce everybody else, Dr. Helser began to talk about me. I knew I was next, and I began to wish I hadn't eaten. Something was wrong with my stomach, and my heart was racing like a windmill.

When Dr. Helser said, "I am happy to present Sam Rizk, an American who had to discover his own country,"

I struggled to my feet and looked blankly in front of me. For a moment that seemed endless my memory was a complete emptiness, and the blur of faces and eyes and clapping hands before me resembled a nightmare.

Then I remembered what I wanted to say.

"Ladies and gentlemen," I started, and I was suddenly terrified by the thickness of my accent. "Please do not think that I am a speaker. I am not a speaker. I am only a dishwater. I mean, I mean, I am only a dishwasher."

Well, everybody laughed so hard I began to wonder if they were ever going to stop. But after that everything became easy. The friendliest thing in the world is a laugh, even when it is at your own expense. I forgot my prepared speech and told my story just the way I had told it to the kids in school: How I was born in Syria and my mother died, leaving me to be cared for by a grandmother. How the death of my grandmother left me a miserable and ragged orphan in war-torn Syria. How I managed to survive by eating raw birds' eggs and roots in the hills. How I learned I was an American citizen. How it took five long, painful years to prove it. How at last I came to America, and how I felt when I saw this vast, rich land with its great farms and teeming cities. How I almost lost America in a packing plant, and how I found it again in a public school. How I appreciated the privileges and opportunities of this great and miraculous land, the friendliness and helpfulness of its people, especially those who had helped me so much in Ames.

When I got through, I sat down and everybody else stood up. They applauded and applauded until Mr. Davis motioned me to stand up, too. I knew they were not applauding me. They were applauding America, the land where something like this could happen to anybody, a land where a man was free, with the help of his fellows, to work out his own destiny. I knew that I was living proof to them of what America was and what America could be. They were proud of a nation because of me. But I could not feel proud. It was a very great and a very humbling experience.

When the meeting broke up, everybody came to shake hands with me. People invited me to their homes. They wanted me to meet their children. They asked me to speak to their clubs. They offered to lend me money to fulfill my ambitions. All this sudden flood of warmth and hospitality, all this friendliness and generosity awakened in me a feeling I had been trying to capture from the first day I landed in America—the feeling that I belonged here, that I was accepted. For the first time I really felt what my passport had tried so hard to suggest and prove: that I was an American, that I belonged to these people and they belonged to me.

Two days later I got my promised promotion. The boss made me a "waitress." But not because of what the newspaper said. He put me on a night job because one of the waiters got drunk and didn't show up for work. It was not so much a promotion as an addition: I continued to wash dishes and scrub floors; waiting on tables was only an added chore.

After eleven o'clock at night, when the last straggling customers had left, the other help went home and I was left in charge until morning. Sometimes I would play at being the whole restaurant crew. When a customer came in I would get his order and shout it back to the kitchen, "Hamburger and coffee on one." Then I would run back to the kitchen, cook the hamburger, and serve it.

Two weeks after my promotion I was fired. The first trouble was the night work. I couldn't get used to sleeping in the daytime, and at night, especially between four and five in the morning, it was all I could do to keep awake. Early one morning, after I had finished my duties, I sat down at a table to steal a bit of rest and fell sound asleep. Presently I awoke. It seemed as if the whole building were shaking. It was my boss. He had me in his powerful paws. He took off my apron and tied it around his own ample waist and began to bustle about, straightening up all the things I had straightened up to show how badly I had neglected my work.

"Go home," he said tersely. "Go home and go to sleep."

I thought I was fired, but I couldn't be sure. I reported

for work the next night, and nobody said anything, so I just stayed on.

But I didn't feel secure. I expected to be booted out any day, and this fear did not help to improve my efficiency in any way.

My dismissal came finally as the result of my failure to understand plain English. I was still having a lot of trouble making out words, especially when people spoke rapidly— and they were always speaking too fast—or when they talked in the listless, unemphatic way of tired people who eat in cafés at midnight. The words slid into each other and ran together until they seemed like one big glob of melted butter. When customers gave me their orders I did not always hear right. They would order a ham sandwich and I would bring them a hamburger. They would ask for fried eggs and I would bring them the Friday special. All this embarrassed me no end and angered the boss enormously.

"What you t'ink," he would say, "we want to fid pipuls not'ing but hash? You t'ink I'm in the garbage business?"

One day after I had served an impatient customer a hot beef sandwich when he had ordered a roast-beef dinner, the boss jerked my apron off and with suppressed profanity hissed, "You go home and sleep, damn you—and stay asleep."

As I trudged back to my room, I was not exactly dejected.

I knew it wouldn't be hard to find another job. Yet I began to wonder if I could keep it. I took stock of my liabilities. I could not speak English, read English, understand English. I could not take orders, could not fill orders. I began to wonder about what Joe had said to me that first day in Ames, "In America, Sam, you can work your way through school." Yes, I thought, you can work your way through school, if you know how to work—enough at least to hold a job.

CHAPTER XIV

Free Shoe Repair for the Poor

WITHIN A FEW DAYS I had found another job shining shoes in a Greek shoe parlor. One of the shoemakers employed here was a rugged Lithuanian called Gus. He was a queer sort of fellow, but I liked him a lot. He would cobble for hours, wrapped in impenetrable silence—that is, in as much silence as his habit of sucking saliva through the leaks around his pipestem would permit. His inseparable companion all day long was this pipe, an ancient and odorous, long-stemmed brier by means of which we were able to keep in touch with the ebb and flow of his inner life. Whenever he got excited about anything, he would blow an immense cloud bank of smoke, within which, his beaming face told us, he found it most congenial to do his thinking and scheming. When the pipe went out we knew he had cooled off and the inner fires were burning low. At such times he gripped the cold pipe firmly between his brown-stained teeth and sucked saliva at a reduced rate of speed.

One day, after smoking his pipe rapturously for some time, Gus took me aside and said, "Tonight you come to my place, Sime. I want it we should talk. Sure?"

"Talk about what?" I asked.

"About you—and me."

"What about you and me?"

"I tell you tonight," he said mysteriously.

"Tell me now," I insisted.

Keeping one eye peeled for the boss, he whispered, "You know what makes the big business here, Sime?"

He paused, and I shook my head.

"You make it."

"Oh no, Gus," I said, "I don't make business. This business was here before I came. They got along fine without me before. They can get along without me again. That's what I'm afraid of. Maybe the boss will find out and fire me."

"No, no, no, Sime," he protested. "You know what makes it the business—more business? You go out and talk. Peepuls like to hear it. They think it great. They fin' out you work here an' they bring it their shoes. That's what makes it the business. But what you get? Just tips and kick in the pants."

"It isn't that bad, Gus. I make thirteen dollars a week, and——"

"Yes, t'irteen dollars the week! You could make fifty, sixty, one hundred dollars the week. You have your own shop. You make big business for yourself."

"But, Gus, I can't do that. I can't repair shoes."

"That's where me come in," he said, and he smiled all over. "You be boss. I be shoemaker. You make goot business. I fix goot shoes. You come by my place downtown tonight. We talk it over."

So that evening I spent in the humble home of my Lithuanian friend. Gus smoked his pipe ardently, and we turned the matter over, studying it from every angle. I began to be really intrigued with the whole idea. One thing I did not consider long, and that was the social position of a shoemaker in America. In Syria a cobbler is low-class, next thing to a beggar. But in this country, I thought, I could repair shoes, be an American businessman, win the respect of my friends and neighbors, maybe even belong to the Rotary Club. Another thing, I would be my own boss. When I worked for other people and made a mistake, they fired me. But when they made mistakes, they did not fire themselves. "If I work for myself," I reasoned out loud, "I will not fire me, will I, Gus, even when I don't like what I do?"

For another thing, I would be freer to go to school. I could spend part of my time in the shop, taking care of the business. The rest of the time I might take courses at the college. The more I turned the plan over in my mind, the more it appealed to me.

There was only one thing wrong with the whole scheme: I had no money. How could I start a business without any capital? Well, I shouldn't say any capital. I had six dollars. But Gus said it would take at least $2,000, and I had no idea of how that much money could be found.

Nevertheless, with the sublime confidence born of a sublimer ignorance, I went after the money and credit necessary to such an undertaking. Within three weeks I was able to open a shop of my own all rigged out with $2,300 worth of tools, machinery, counters, shelves, and bootblack equipment—and no business.

Our opening day was a Friday in early September. Summer school was over; the regular college term was still three weeks off. We couldn't have started out at a more inauspicious time.

Gus and I talked the situation over.

"No business, Sime. No business for t'ree week," Gus said gloomily, drawing an apathetic puff from his pipe.

"Gus," I said, "we can't go for three weeks without business. I have to pay you wages. There is rent and installment payments and all the rest. Besides, I have to eat. If we have to pay money out for three weeks without taking any in, we'll be broke in less time than it took to get started."

"I got it idee, Sime." Gus's face was beaming, and he was puffing on his pipe with fruitful vigor. "I got it idee."

"What is it, Gus?"

"It's a goot idee, a wonderful idee, Sime. You wouldn't t'ink of it in million years."

That was Gus's way, and I sometimes lost patience with him. Puffing away behind his fertile pipe, he would suddenly glow all over with self-generated enthusiasm. His face would light up from within, and his brier bowl would start belching enormous clouds of smoke. He would draw and blow and suck saliva to keep it from running down his chin. It sounded as if he were eating hot soup in Lithuania. When the vapors got thick enough he would say, "I got it idee, Sime," and then he would tease me along for hours, lapsing into long silences, once in a while breaking out in a new wreath of smiles, "Have you t'ink of it, Sime? No. You wouldn't t'ink of it in million years." I could have booted him.

This time, however, he was more than usually anxious to tell me.

"Sime, you know kids in school. That's the place to start business. Those kids help you. You tell 'em you have shoeshop and"—Gus snapped his powerful fingers convincingly—"lots of business."

That very day I arranged to go from class to class, telling my little friends about my shop and inviting them to bring their broken-down boots and shoes to our new, up-to-date shoe hospital. It worked like magic. By late Saturday afternoon we had twenty-four dollars' worth of business on the shelves, and Gus puffed his pipe more serenely. "Sime," he rejoiced expansively, "I have goot idee, eh? You wouldn't t'ink of it in million years. No sir, you wouldn't t'ink of it in million years."

In late September the campus began to stir. The big cars and the middle-sized cars and the red-and-yellow-bestickered jallopies began to roll in, piled high with bags and trunks, bristling with tennis racquets, golf clubs, and noisy students. We ran an ad in the college paper: "This is the most modern shoe clinic in town. Our patients are returned in excellent health, those dyed included." We appointed a student agent in each dormitory to solicit business. The agents distributed a thousand printed cards on the campus giving the holder five free shines at our shop. That meant 5,000 free shines—but we didn't think of that until all the cards had been passed out.

Soon business was booming. We had to hire three extra shiners to take care of the rush in free-shine business, and two extra shoemakers to help Gus turn out repaired shoes. Later we installed a telephone and bought a secondhand motorcycle with sidecar to provide our customers with free delivery service.

For several months the shop kept me so busy I had no

time to think about improving my English—or at least no time to do anything about it. Now, with a steady stream of business and things better organized, I managed to find, or rather make, time to learn again.

One of my shoemakers was a Syrian student at the college, and I paid him to read to me an hour a day while I cobbled. For every book I gave him a quarter; and for every new word I learned, a cent. Sometimes I learned fifty new words a week. Here was really a fine illustration of American democracy—two Syrian orphans each making it possible for the other to become a useful and independent citizen, one by teaching the language, the other by giving him a job.

Not only students but teachers, too, and almost everyone in the community came in to help and encourage me. Jim Wilson brought me to speak to his English classes. Others brought me books and magazine articles and took me to the theater and concerts in Des Moines. And many of my happiest memories are of evenings spent in Ames homes romping with the family or discussing politics and economic problems.

Economic problems, in fact, were beginning to get a lot of attention just then. There had been a stock-market crash, bankruptcies, foreclosures, suicides, and a condition people called a depression. Talking about it was an obsession with some people. They never came into the shop without blam-

ing the government or Wall Street or the Jews or the
radicals for all the troubles the country was having. To me
a lot of this discussion was like the talk about prohibition,
not nearly as bad as the opposition painted it. All around
me were the plainest proofs of prosperity. I could not ignore
them. They belied the gloomy headlines and editorials in
the newspapers and the complaints of the grocer and the
landlord. People still drove fine cars, ate plenty of good
food, dressed as elegantly as ever, lived in the same fine,
rich-looking houses, even took trips to Europe. Nothing
that I could see had dwindled or burned or blown up.
Everything stood just as before—the whole magnificent
material achievement of America—the great buildings of
the college, the well-kept business district, the beautiful
homes and the rich farm land all around. And everywhere
in the country, I imagined, it was much the same. How
could there be a depression? When people talked about
hard times and poverty, I was confused. Sometimes I was
indignant. "What do you mean, hard times?" I said to a
grumbling friend of mine. "What do you mean, the country is going to the dogs? You ought to see hard times where
I came from. There's real hard times—hunger, scarcity,
misery, and rags. When you don't have crops, or the plague
comes, or an army raids your village and loots and destroys
your homes—that's poverty. But here people are actually
complaining because of overabundance, because they have

raised and made too much. Can you explain that to me? Is that poverty?"

Then, one day, I saw the depression with my own eyes. It was a cold December day, and I had gone down to the city hall to pay my utility bills. And there on the steps I got my first glimpse of the depression, a sight I had never expected to see in America: a boy, ten or twelve years old, skinny and ragged, quivering like a leaf in the raw wind.

"Hello," I said.

"Hello."

"Are you cold?"

"Boy, I'll say!"

I looked at his shoes. From habit.

"Let me see your shoes."

He held them up, sticking his foot straight out so I couldn't see any more than before.

"No, let me see the bottoms."

He turned his foot over.

"My goodness, look at the flesh. Don't you have any other shoes?"

"No, these are all the shoes I got."

"What are you doing here?"

"Waiting for somebody."

"Do you have to see them now?"

"No."

"Well, you see, I'm a shoemaker. If you'll go out to the

shop with me I'll put a pair of soles on those shoes. I'll bring you back. Do you want to do that?"

He hesitated a moment and then said, "O.K."

I never saw such a miserable pair of shoes in my life, all wet inside and the welts so frayed and rotten you couldn't make a sole hang to them. The tongues were torn out and the shoestrings tied in a dozen knots. We repaired the shoes the best we could, put some inner soles in and new laces. We gave him a handful of laces for his sisters, too, and then I took him home down by the tracks.

On the way back to the shop I couldn't get that boy off my mind. There must be other youngsters just like this, and grown men and women, too, their fathers and mothers, tramping around in the winter slush with shoes that leaked cold and water and all kinds of terrible sickness. What could be done about it?

One Saturday afternoon I decided to drop in to see my friend, Father Burroughs, rector of the Episcopal church, who lived just three blocks from my shop.

"Father," I said, "I want to do something about this, but I don't know just what. Maybe if people who are better off could bring in their old, discarded shoes I could repair them for these poor people; but I don't know how to go about it."

"That's a splendid idea, Sam," he said, "but do you think you can afford to do it?"

"Sure, I can afford it. Why not? When I was hard up,

other people not as well off as I am now helped me. All I want to know is how I can get in touch with people who have old shoes to give away."

"Sam, if you really want to do it, I can help you with an announcement from the pulpit in the morning. I'll bet you can get a dozen pair of shoes out of my parish alone."

"Do you think the other preachers would announce it, too?"

"You bet they would. Why don't you talk to them, Sam?"

So that afternoon I ran all over town, talking to the preachers. They were all very kind and receptive and pledged their wholehearted support. I felt a deeper satisfaction over this than I did over getting started in business. I began to feel I was earning my way in America. This wasn't charity at all: just paying something back.

I wasn't really prepared for the avalanche that descended upon my shop Monday morning. The response of the people was instantaneous and overwhelming. They brought shoes of every description; men's shoes, women's shoes, children's shoes, even baby shoes. They brought them tied up in newspapers, in paper bags and cartons, in bushel baskets and gunny sacks, and tied together in strings. Some of them must have canvassed their neighborhoods.

I had not told Gus about any of this, and I very nearly lost a good shoemaker over it. As the shoes piled up on the counter, he was beside himself with delight. His face was wreathed in smiles and smoke, and he fairly danced a jig as he cried, "Lots of business, Sime, lots of business. I tell you we ketch the business. You go out and talk, make friends; we ketch the business."

Well, I had talked, but, from Gus's point of view, to the wrong people.

When he started to rip soles from the old shoes I told him. And he blew up.

"What! You crazy? You fix shoes for poor peepul. Free? You're poor peepul yourself. Is anybody poor like you? You owe money—two t'ousand dollar. Does any poor peepul owe that much? No. You are the poor one. They should fix your shoes, dammit. I t'ink you crazy."

He banged his hammer on the bench and glared at me with unbelief.

The rest of the day he was sullen. Every time he looked at me, disgust and scorn were written all over his face. All over mine, too, for I was trying to be just as disgusted with him.

An hour before closing time Gus took off his apron and without a word left the shop, hunched over his pipe, which had gone out. He didn't return. I was plenty worried. Hundreds of old shoes to repair and no master shoemaker. But maybe he would get over it and come back. After all, he hadn't said anything about quitting.

I began to wonder if I had gotten myself into something

too big to handle. The shelves and counters were loaded with shoes. They overflowed into the back room where I lived. They were pushed under the bed, looped in chains over the backs of chairs, and piled in the corners.

I lay awake a long time that night, worrying about old shoes and Gus and huge leather bills and poor people without shoes, and then I dropped off to sleep dreaming about old shoes and Gus and huge leather bills and poor people without shoes. The poor people, ragged and barefooted, started marching in a long, dreary procession across fields covered with ice and snow. Marching beside them were empty old shoes with their worn toes turned up, their soles flapping loosely, and the twisted, knotty laces dragging in the snow. Then the dream changed. The people and the shoes were marching into a city. At an intersection, standing right in the middle of the street, directing traffic, was Gus. He had on a funny policeman's cap, the kind police wear in Beirut, and he was smoking his pipe enthusiastically and waving his arms. He directed all the poor, barefooted people down one street, and all the shoes down the other. "Lots o' business, Sime," he shouted. "Lots o' business. I wouldn't t'ink of it in million years. No sir, I wouldn't t'ink of it in million years."

I awoke and turned on the lights. My head was throbbing with thoughts. Now I remembered reading somewhere about full grain bins on the farms and hungry people on the bread lines, about bursting warehouses and empty pantries, glutted factories and underfed children, and how none of them could get together because something, a Mr. X, was keeping them apart. I began to wonder, who is Gus? Who is directing all the hunger down one street and all the food down the other street, all the bare feet here and all the empty shoes there?

Shoes! Every time I looked at a pile of shoes it made my heart sick. It was as if they asked me a million questions: "Who is going to repair me? Who is going to wear me? Where is the money coming from? How long do you think you can stay in business? Do you think Gus will come back?" I had to get those darn shoes out of sight. I got up, pulled on a pair of pants, and went to the basement. There, behind the furnace, were all sorts of paper cartons and wooden boxes. I dragged them upstairs and sorted the shoes into them and carried them all downstairs.

It was about four o'clock. The night policeman walking his beat came to the door. I unlocked it and stepped into the street, deserted except for a few parked cars. The air was raw, and I asked the cop to come in and warm up.

"Get your days and nights mixed, Sam?" he asked, stamping the snow off of his shoes.

"No, I've got too many shoes."

"Too many shoes? What's the matter? Too much business?"

"No. Too much monkey business. I've got hundreds, maybe a thousand, shoes to fix for poor people—and no poor people. And my shoemaker has left me—I think."

"Say that again. I don't get it."

So I told him the whole story from the beginning.

"Why don't you take your shoes down to the city hall, Sam? The Social Service Bureau will take care of 'em. They get all the needy people down there. If anybody needs shoes, they can fit them and then send the shoes out here for you to repair. I wouldn't fix them until I found somebody they fit."

"Thank you, thank you, Mr. Policeman. I'll do that. Thank you very much!"

Early the next morning I unloaded the shoes at the city hall. The Social Service people were amazed, but they seemed very glad to get them. That was a big relief. I went back to the shop, determined to find Gus.

Gus was back. He had his apron on and was working away at the stitcher, blowing smoke all over the place.

"Gus," I said, "you can't smoke so darn much in here. You'll drive all the business away."

"Where's the shoes, Sime?"

"What do you care? They're gone, aren't they?"

"Sime," he said softly, with a kind of fatherly tenderness in his voice, "you know I don't quit you. I don't care you fix it shoes for poor peepul. I want to help it poor peepul, too. But you can't make living fix shoes for not'ing. If you help poor peepul too much you get poor yourself. Then who going to help you?"

"Gus," I said, "I'm going to use those old shoes to learn shoe repairing. When I get good enough, I'm going to fire you. Then I'll ruin my business in my own way."

Gus only grinned. He knew I would never do that.

A month or so later a well-dressed, salesman-like gentleman came into the shop.

"I am Mr. Rich from Kortum & Keane," he said. That was the house that had set me up in business, and, of course, I still bought all my leather supplies from them.

"The company sent me here to investigate your business."

Investigate my business? What was this? Why should anyone want to investigate my business?

"Don't be alarmed," he reassured me, "but rumors have come to the company that you have been violating the ethics of the trade."

"What have I done?" I asked uneasily.

"Well, the complaint, Mr. Rizk—and please don't think I'm passing judgment—the complaint is that you are using unethical advertising methods to build up your business."

"Yes?" I swallowed hard.

"The company had a letter protesting against your free

shoe-repair service. It said you were capitalizing on the good will of the people, that you have been using the churches to advertise your business, that you are using charity as a means of drumming up trade."

"Was there anything else?" I asked.

"Well, yes. They don't like the way you give talks to the college classes. They say you are taking unfair advantage of your story to make business for yourself."

"You mean I should quit repairing shoes free and giving those talks?" My head was running with thoughts. One of them I was absolutely sure of: if it came to a choice, I would surrender my business before I would give up the opportunity of speaking to young Americans about America.

"No, that isn't what I think," the man said in answer to my question.

"What do you think?" I asked.

"Of course, I can't speak for the company, because they have the final say-so in the matter, but my opinion is that it's a great idea. In times like these we'd all be better off if we helped each other more. I've talked to people in the community, and they think so, too. When I report to the company, I'm going to recommend that they continue your credit."

But now I had a new worry. Maybe the company will not see it the way the salesman does. Maybe my credit *will* be shut off. Maybe my competitors are right. Telling my story to the public does bring business to my shop. Repairing shoes free for the poor does make good will for me. Is it unethical, or isn't it? I didn't know. I just waited and worried.

Finally a bulky letter came from the company. I was almost afraid to open it. It contained two pages of typewritten material and some advertising matter. I got out the dictionary and began to read it—the letter. What it said relieved my fears, and I began to think I worried too much about everything. First, it commended me in the most glowing language for my "philanthropic spirit." Second, it invited me to address the National Shoe Dealers at their convention in Chicago the last of March. They wanted me to explain this business of free shoe repairing for the poor.

A few weeks after the convention I learned that over three hundred shoeshops in the United States and Canada had pledged to devote one day each month to the free repair of shoes for the unemployed in their communities.

I thought: "What will be the next miracle to come out of this America? Here am I, a humble, obscure shoemaker. I start an idea and it goes all over the country. That is one of the marvelous things about free America. Anybody—a carpenter, a butcher, a grocer, or a housewife—can originate a scheme for democratic improvement or service, and if it has value, it will catch on all over the country, become the property, the working capital, of all the people—and it doesn't need any push from the government. The people just do it themselves. And nobody has to like an idea just because somebody else likes it, just because it has some kind of official approval. You can even co-operate with a plan and not like it—and say so."

Several months after the Chicago convention I went to Des Moines on business and stopped in one of those beautiful, modern shoe emporiums to have a shine. In the window there was a sign, with an emblem underneath, which read something like this: "We devote one day each month to the free repair of shoes for the unfortunate and unemployed in our city." Curious, I asked the owner about it.

"Yeah," he snorted, "we co-operate. But it's a hell of a business. You know those —— —— slum trashes don't only want their shoes repaired free. They call up and want to know if we run a free delivery service."

"How'd you get the idea?" I inquired.

"Oh, some damfool Syrian shoemaker in Ames thought it up."

I had some more questions to ask, but thought I had better not. Anyway, this is a free country. You don't have to like anybody's idea, not even a damfool Syrian shoemaker's.

CHAPTER XV

How Not to Cure a Depression

As THE DEPRESSION GREW WORSE I saw that not only was my own security threatened, but that of my neighbors and nearly everyone else in America, and that people were grumbling and complaining more and more. Then I had to fight to keep alive my faith in America. Just as I had thought of Syria as a land of eternal poverty, the helpless victim of foreign governments, taxgatherers and locusts, so had I pictured America as a land of eternal riches, where there was so much wealth lying around that it was a disgrace to be poor, where it was possible for everyone to be free from hunger and poverty forever.

So when I found hunger at my door in America, my fear and despondency were greater than they had ever been in Syria. In that land my poverty and wretchedness had never seemed altogether hopeless. I had thought, "Someday I will escape all this. Someday I will go to America." But now I was in America, and where could I escape to?

What added to my discouragement was that millions of Americans were actually in a worse plight than I was. They were so poor they didn't know where next month's rent or even next week's groceries were coming from, and it was not their fault. They wanted to work and couldn't find work. The factories which had employed them wanted to sell goods, but they couldn't find enough customers. The banks were glutted with money, but where were the borrowers?

There seemed to be no natural or logical way to explain all this. There was no plague, no drought, only rich cornfields, and everybody in Iowa seemed to have enough to eat. When I read of people going hungry and long bread lines in the cities, while potatoes were being burned in Texas and huge piles of oranges dumped in California—well, all that twisted my reason just as hunger had twisted my stomach in Syria. When we were hungry in Syria it was because we did not have enough. But here people said there was hunger because we had too much. I could not understand that.

Things got much worse in Ames. The state treasury of Iowa ran out of funds and had to pay the teachers and professors at the state college in tax warrants. Then the Ames banks closed, and the teachers couldn't cash their warrants. One day a professor came to my shop to call for a pair of shoes. He dumped a dollar's worth of pennies on the counter, and I asked him where he had gotten all the chicken feed.

"I'm a bank robber now, Sam," he explained, and I thought I detected tears in his eyes.

"A bank robber? You can't rob busted banks, can you?" I said, trying to make a joke.

"Yes, Sam, you can rob some busted banks," he said, managing a smile. "I robbed Jimmy's bank this morning. Believe it or not, that's all the cash we've got."

I could hardly believe it—my friends breaking their children's savings banks to stave off starvation.

"Listen," I said. "You don't have to pay for these shoes now. You need those pennies for bread."

"No, Sam, the grocer will carry me. You take the money. We'll get along. We have people. You don't. You'll need this worse than we will."

When he walked out, I was so mad I could have chewed leather. But whom was I mad at? I didn't know. Whom could I be mad at? I remembered my dream the night I slept with all those shoes in the back of the shop, the night Gus sent all the barefooted people down one street and all the empty shoes down another street. Who is Gus? I wondered. Who is responsible for all this fear and misery in rich, powerful, kindly America, this big brother to the world who had sent meat and grain to starving Europe, this America that had sent food and medical supplies and Red

Cross angels to Syria after the World War? I was utterly astonished and confounded.

So I went over to the college and enrolled as a special student in two courses, one in American history, the other in economics. I thought maybe this would throw some light on my bewilderment. But the professors were just as puzzled as I was. Yet, like everyone else, they had their theories and remedies.

The young businessmen of Ames formed an organization to improve business and serve the community. They invited me to join. We met for dinner from time to time and listened to speeches on the cause and cure of depressions.

On one occasion, I remember, a highly successful businessman urged upon us a cure for the depression with such great and flawless eloquence that we were unanimously moved to adopt it. "The depression was caused by bad psychology," he said. "Our thinking has been all wrong, too distrustful, too pessimistic, too depressing. We thought and talked our way into this depression. We can think and talk our way out of it. If every businessman in America will pledge himself to absolute silence on the subject of panics, depressions, and economic collapses, the resulting business improvement will show up on your cash registers within two weeks. Silence, my friends, will again prove to be golden."

Then he passed out to each member of the organization

a fancy handkerchief with words something to this effect printed on it: "Give me to the next bozo who boohoos about the depression and tell him to shut up or dry up."

I took my handkerchief home and gave it to the next-door grocer. He laughed at me, but for two weeks I was enthusiastically silent, and for two weeks I kept a hopeful eye on the cash register. Never once did I mention the word "depression." When other people spoke of it I changed the subject. To all the classroom radicals, calamity howlers, and armchair critics I rudely turned a deaf ear.

Though I was anxious, after a few days, to learn what kind of business my friends were enjoying as a result of this concerted crusade of silence, I was afraid to mention it for fear of breaking my pledge and endangering the whole plan. So I kept still and all the other members kept still.

After a while it became apparent that somebody had been talking. We should have known better. It is impossible to impose universal silence on any subject in the United States. One of my friends, an incorrigible enthusiast of the idea, said later, "Maybe in Italy you could work it, where one man can make the whole darn country shut up at once. But in this country we have too doggone much free speech."

So that plan failed, but it did not quench my optimism. Another speaker came along and proposed a solution which must have been worked out with the help of a brain trust, it was so bad. But like all the rest I fell for it, lock, stock, and barrel, or perhaps I should say, stalk, husk, and ear, since it had to do with a new way of using up the corn surplus in the country.

This fellow was less famous and more modest than the other. To us businessmen he said, "The answer to the depression is simple. This is an agricultural state. Our depression is at bottom an agricultural depression. If we can restore agriculture, we can restore business. The problem then reduces itself to this: what is the matter with agriculture? Well, you know the answer to that. The farmer has produced too much. Our trouble today is corn trouble, too much corn, corn that cannot be absorbed by the market. What the great state of Iowa needs to do, to put it surgically, is to trim her corn. How can we businessmen do anything about that? Well, we all have furnaces, and every winter we burn thousands of tons of coal imported from other states. When our dollars go for coal, they work and create prosperity in Pennsylvania and West Virginia, but the great state of Iowa goes begging. Suppose now we all agree to burn two or three tons of corn mixed with coal and keep some of those dollars at home. Do you see what that will do?"

Yes, we saw. It was beautiful. So simple. So inexpensive. Yes, even profitable. Why hadn't someone thought of it before? You could burn things up and actually be money ahead. Wonderful, ingenious, miraculous—and crazy!

But the plain, bald insanity of it didn't strike home until later. When my truckload of corn—leaves, stalks, husks, and ears—was delivered, one of the classroom radicals from the college, a perfervid young man who had been organizing a local branch of the League for Industrial Democracy, happened to be in my shop.

"Going to raise hogs in the basement, Sam?" he asked jokingly.

"No, you don't raise hogs in town. I'm going to mix this corn with coal and burn it in the furnace."

He stared at me with revolution in his eyes. "Oh, you're going to raise hell."

"What do you mean, raise hell? This is going to bring us back to normalcy."

"Normalcy, nuts! You know what you're doing, Sam? You're stoking the fires of hell, stoking the fires of revolt in this country—with corn. How long do you think the hungry people are going to stand for this kind of nonsense? People stand in bread lines for hours to get a crust to eat, and you shovel good, rich, yellow corn into the furnace. Is that the way you expect to restore prosperity? If that's the road back to normalcy, then I hope to God I'm abnormal."

"But you don't understand, Bill," I said. "We're helping the farmer to get rid of his surplus so he will get better prices for his grain and will have more money to spend in town. Everybody will be better off when the farmer gets back his purchasing power. That's what the speaker said."

"What speaker?"

So I told him about the speech we had heard and the pledge we had taken and all the corn we were going to burn in our furnaces just in Ames alone that winter.

"This country is crazy, Sam, plumb crazy," he said, and his voice trembled with emotion. "Why, it's a damnable outrage to decency and common sense. Think of it! People expect to get rich by destroying the country's crops, its real wealth. They think they are going to be better off by making the country worse off. Listen, Sam, you could burn all the money in the world and we wouldn't be one whit worse off, but you burn all the food in the world and see where we wind up."

"But how are you going to buy food if you don't have money?"

"That isn't the question at all. The question is, how are you going to buy food if you burn it? The trouble with the country, Sam, is we've substituted a fiction called money for the real, solid things of life."

"What's the matter with you and money?" I asked. "Don't you get along with it?"

"Heck, you can't get along without it. But, Sam, money isn't the real thing, and when people start burning the real thing to get the stuff that only stands for the real thing, then there's something screwy about our thinking and the whole rotten system that makes our thinking so crooked and greedy."

I wasn't convinced. "Who do you think you are, an economist?" I taunted him.

"Economist, hell! I'm not one of them soothsayers."

We argued some more and got nowhere. After all, wasn't the logic of economic law on my side? Hadn't the speaker made it plain? We had too much corn, so the bottom had fallen out of the market. To restore the market, get rid of the surplus corn. Then the price goes up, the farmer has more money to spend, and everybody is better off. Plain as the nose on your face.

That evening I went to the basement as usual to fire the furnace. I threw on several shovelfuls of coal and then turned to the corn, which rested like a huge tangled shock on top of the coal. I picked up a stalk, shucked off an ear and husked it out. A beautiful ear, fat and hefty in the hand, almost a foot long, it seemed, with gleaming yellow kernels standing in straight, neat rows like soldiers at attention. Food this was, good, rich, priceless, life-giving food, food to keep the sharp fangs of famine out of the belly. Then the full force of the crime I was about to commit dawned upon me. It was a kind of murder, that's what it was—slow murder, the slow, creeping, cramping death of

starvation, and I had pledged to be a party to it. Somewhere
in the world tonight—maybe in the old country—a life
might be saved with this food; perhaps the life of a little
ragged boy out there, grubbing in the stingy earth as I once
did. My hand trembled. Life and death—here in my hand.
I thought of those World War days in Syria—it all came
back now real as life—when we scratched and scrabbled in
the hills, in the dull gray earth, for just one shriveled root
to eat, when we scoured the fields for a few grains of wheat
to still the twisting pain in the stomach. Why, there had
been people in those days who clawed the putrescence of
dead bodies out of their shallow graves; parents who had
killed their own children for food. Horror upon horror,
ghosts of yesterday, sprouted from those fat, mocking
kernels in my hand. I couldn't stop them.

You see, in Syria I was taught by the people and by the
earth, and more by the earth than by the people, that it is
a sin to trample on a crust of bread or even to throw it down
where someone else might trample it. There were things
that were burned in my memory. I remembered the day my
schoolmaster asked me to nail up a curtain over the window
in our little school. I had just stepped up on his desk to
reach the nail when, in a sudden, gentle gesture, he lifted
me to the floor. Overcome with consternation and apolo-
gizing profusely, he removed a loaf of bread from a drawer
—his lunch—and laid it on top of the desk. Then, kneeling

before the entire school and beckoning me to do the same, he made the Sign of the Cross and asked God's forgiveness for our unwitting sacrilege. I hadn't touched the bread, but it had been in the desk under my feet.

Then I remembered the woman in my village who accidentally spilled some flour on the ground before the *tanur* and how carefully she had gathered it all up and tied it in a cloth, saying, "We have committed a sin. Someday God will make us pick up every wasted grain, one by one, between the lids of our sinful eyes."

So sacred is bread in the lands where it is never to be had in plenty. . . .

But this was America. Could it be different here? Was bread so abundant and human need so rare that food could be wasted without penalty or sacrilege or shame? I thought of the coal miners digging in the mountains of Pennsylvania and West Virginia, or rather no longer digging, for they were out of work by the thousands. Could they eat their coal for food the way we burned this corn for fuel? How would they get money to live if we quit buying their coal? Was it right for us to think of our prosperity first and forget them? Could we indeed ever hope to have or even deserve real prosperity so long as we threw God's bounty back into His face? Questions and more questions, which answered themselves, throbbed in my brain, lashing my conscience into protest against this wicked, unjustified waste of the very stuff of earthly life.

Sick at heart, I tossed the ear of corn into the mouth of the furnace. Hungry tongues of flame leaped up and licked at it greedily. "It is insanity," I thought, "a confession of human madness, the final proof of our common stupidity. The worst of all is that we are helpless, caught like flies in a net of evil not of our own making. Our society is a monstrous web from which we cannot escape, in which we cannot find security or happiness or any pleasurable success; a web of stocks and bonds, of money and mortgages, of debits and credits; we are all caught in it, struggling to free our wings from want and only getting more entangled, unintentionally hurting and destroying each other in a senseless, futile struggle to live."

I have never been a fatalist, but I was close to being one then. If even in rich, abundant America men were fated to poverty, then the earth was hopeless. One could only pray that that other Heaven might be better, and I was not yet ready to transfer my interest to that.

CHAPTER XVI

Marvelous Freedom of Speech

"I FEEL SORRY FOR YOU FOREIGNERS," the campus cynic who loafed in my shop would say. "You are so naïve, so foolishly optimistic. You work so hard in this little shop. You actually think that by hard work and study you will get somewhere. You still believe that old line that America is the land of freedom and opportunity and all that stuff. Well, it used to be, but not any more. The frontiers are gone, and the freedom and opportunity are gone. Now we are all slaves in the hands of sixty-two millionaire families, and there's no way to escape them."

Sometimes I was almost in a mood to agree with him. The depression became a black and ugly thing. You could see it on the faces of the people. Businesses failed, banks closed, the student enrollment at the college dropped off. Finally I had to lay off all my help, all except one part-time shoeshiner.

Even then the overhead was more than the business could bear, and at last there seemed nothing to do to avert foreclosure. Only two more days now, and I needed $100 to pay an overdue note. I counted my petty cash. There was just $23. Never free from poverty, not even in America, I thought.

I spent five of the twenty-three dollars for a wedding present. One of my friends, a young man who had recently graduated from the college, was getting married, and he had invited me to attend the ceremony in a little town about sixty miles from Ames. When I reached his home my face must have looked more like a funeral than a wedding, for Larry, the groom, noticed it at once. He pulled me off to one side and said, "Sam, something's bothering you. What is it?"

"Oh, nothing much, Larry," I said. "Just a little business trouble."

"That's bad these days. Is there anything I can help you with?"

"Oh no. I don't want any help. Things'll work out all right," I said.

"Now wait a minute, Sam. I've never seen you look like this before. I know there's something really wrong. You know I don't want to meddle in your business, but if you need any help, say so. I'll be glad to do what I can."

"It's no use insisting, Larry. I've got to get myself out of this jam. Don't bother yourself about my troubles at your wedding."

"Listen, if it'll do you any good to get it off your chest, I'm listening."

So I told him how bad things were looking for my business—note overdue, no money to pay it with, and all that.

"Wait a minute," he said, leaping to his feet and patting my shoulder. "Just wait a minute—stay right here. I'll be back." And before I could recover from my astonishment he had bolted through the door and disappeared.

In five minutes he was back. "Here, take this, Sam," he said and slipped a piece of paper into my hand. It was a check for $100.

"Where did you get this?" I asked, more astonished than ever.

"From the old man."

"The old man? Who's the old man?"

"My dad. I told him about you, and he wrote the check, said you could pay it back any way you wanted to, all at once or a little at a time."

"But, gosh, Larry, I can't take this. I don't even know your old man. What if my shop closes up? He might never get his money back."

"Don't be stubborn, Sam. If you don't use it, your shop *will* close up. Take it and forget it."

"What does your old man do?"

"He's a farmer. He lives in Colorado and came here for the wedding."

"A farmer? He must be a pretty good farmer to be able to write a big check like that—and for a stranger, too. I'd like to meet your old man."

So I met the old man—a big, rugged, ruddy-faced man, with the perpetual lines of kindliness engraved on his weather-beaten face. And he was dressed as elegantly as a banker.

I asked him about his farms in Colorado.

"I don't have any farms in Colorado. I'm a retired farmer. I just live there. My farms are all here in Iowa. Colorado is a good state to live in, nice climate and all that, but it doesn't have the farm land this state has."

"You must make pretty good money from your farms."

"Well, we used to, but not any more. These Iowa farms used to be gold mines, but that's all changed since the bottom went out of the market."

Just then some more guests arrived, two of Larry's old-maid aunts, retired schoolteachers they were, and a debonair young businessman from Mason City, who called himself a Socialist.

The old man resumed discussion of the grain and live-stock market, telling how the freight rates exceeded the price of hogs and how once he had shipped hides and received a bill of eight dollars, which was the amount the

hides fell short of paying the shipping charges. He told
of the difficulties of raising money to pay the mortgages,
the interest on borrowed money, and the payments on
machinery.

"The Republican party got the country into this fix," the
Mason City businessman said.

"No, it didn't. Wall Street did that," Larry's father
asserted.

"Wall Street or the Republican party. What's the difference? Wall Street's got a strangle hold on the Republicans,
and they run the party to suit themselves. When they win
an election, they run the country to suit themselves. That's
what's been wrong with us for the last dozen years. First
Harding and Teapot Dome, then Coolidge and do-noth-
ing, and now Hoover and depression."

Here was a good argument going. I listened closely,
thinking I might find out what was wrong with my business.

The old man was warming up. "The trouble with you
radicals is, you never want to face a fact. But take a good
look at this fact: Iowa is a farm state, isn't it? And Iowa is
a Republican state, isn't it? Where do you get the idea,
then, that Wall Street runs the Republican party? It's
just as much a farmer's party as the Democratic party—
yes, and more so."

"Ah, Wall Street is smart, smart enough to fool the

farmers, yes, and the working people, too," averred the
Socialist businessman. "Wall Street knows there's only
one way to get power and that's to get votes, farm votes and
labor votes. They have to hoodwink you farmers into believing that the Republican party is the farmer's party, and
they have to hoodwink the laboring man into thinking the
Republican party is the laboring man's party. So they always dangle nice, juicy bait before both of them, and both
of them are suckers enough to get hooked. But when the
big boys get into power, what does the farmer get? You
ought to know. The bottom knocked out of everything he
sells, and the ceiling blown off of everything he buys. And
what does the workingman get? Two cars in every garage?
Two chickens in every pot? Oh no! All he gets is a lot of
Republican baloney—the depression is a state of mind and
all that bunk."

"You talk as if the Republican party was a closed conspiracy against the public interest," Larry's father retorted.
"What about Borah and Norris? They're always jumping
over the traces. And what about Brookhart and La Fol-
lette? . . ."

"Sons of wild jackasses, all of them," cried the Socialist.
"And why are they called sons of wild jackasses? Because
they won't join the conspiracy. They want to be in the
party, but won't be of it. They're——"

"Sure, they're irregular, which proves my point. The Republican party is just like any political party, a clash of interests. You're bound to get disagreement, but that only proves nobody has absolute control of the party. No policy can be worked for the exclusive benefit of one part of the party. Now take the way the Reconstruction Finance Corporation works——"

"Yes," interrupted the Mason City man, "just take the Reconstruction Finance Corporation. That's a darn good name for it. Who are they reconstructing? Are they reconstructing the farmer? No. Or the workingman? No. Are they even reconstructing the small businessman? Not so's you can notice it. They're reconstructing the big financiers. The whole thing smells of a conspiracy of the moneyed class against the public interest from the word go. Of course, they have a beautiful theory. They say if they help the big shots, the benefits will percolate down to the little guys."

"Well, what's wrong with that?" Larry's father queried, his eyes twinkling. "If you feed the horses, the sparrows will eat."

Everybody laughed at that, and the tension of the argument eased for the moment. But the businessman came right back, still chuckling over the old man's joke: "Yes, that's the trouble with the Republicans. They think of the masses as a flock of sparrows who ought to be satisfied with the leavings. The real Republican leaders are the money-bags who operate behind the scenes. They think of themselves as a special ruling class, a privileged aristocracy, and they think of the masses as a big swill barrel out of which to fatten themselves."

"That's right, Ed," Larry chimed in. "The Republican party has become so arrogant, so filthy and corrupt, so darn drunk with power that it's ruined the country, the banking system, the farmer, the workingman and industry, and darn near ruined itself. It hasn't shown any honest interest in the common people since Teddy Roosevelt. Four more years of Republican rule is enough to ruin heaven, let alone the rest of the country."

I was filled with astonishment. I looked at Larry's father and then back at Larry. Their faces were flushed with excitement. I looked for the old man to rise up and show his authority. He did rise up, stretching his magnificent, rugged frame almost to the ceiling, it seemed. "Yes," he said, "and the Democrats do such a good job raising hell about the bad job the Republicans are doing that the devil's thinking of becoming their next presidential candidate."

We all laughed heartily and stood up, too. The old man put one arm around Larry, reached across his vest with the other and pulled out a watch. "Well, son," he said, "it's about time we were getting married. We're due at the church in half an hour."

Imagine my astonishment at that. It was as if you saw a fuse burn right up to a keg of powder and then quietly snuff out without an explosion. Here were a father and a son disagreeing over their government almost as violently as some Syrian families did over whom they wanted to be oppressed by, but instead of disowning and denouncing each other, they just go on affectionately calling each other "son" and "old man."

"This is the real America," I thought as I drove back to Ames that night. "What if I am poor? Why, with such a spirit, even the poorest man in America is richer than the richest European."

On top of helping me to save my shop, that family gave me a clue to a new appreciation of America. My first astonishment in America had been at the outside facts—the high buildings, well-dressed crowds, countless automobiles, rich farms, and magnificent schools. My bigger astonishments were at the inside truths about my country.

But in spite of this new slant, I was hardly prepared for the strange things which happened in the presidential campaign that fall. Roosevelt was running against Hoover. It seemed almost unbelievable to me that the head of this vast country had to appeal to me and my shoeshiner and the grocer next door in order to stay in the White House. As the campaign grew hotter I was always imagining that President Hoover would call out the Army to crush those who were hurling accusations at him. One of my neighbors would say harsh things against the President right before the corner cop. I was astonished to realize that he couldn't be thrown into jail for criticizing the head of the government. Gradually it dawned on me that in America you can't arrest anybody for being dissatisfied with the government, because the government belongs to the people.

On election day I met the personnel director of the college at the polls. I thought he would challenge my right to vote. What right had I, a poor, stupid peasant, an ignorant immigrant, to match my vote against a scholar's knowledge? Instead, he greeted me with a smile. It seemed perfectly natural to him that I, Salom Rizk, a Syrian shoemaker, should be helping to choose the President of the United States.

I remember during that campaign how the newspaper cartoons by "Ding"—J. N. Darling—ridiculed Roosevelt. When Roosevelt won, I expected him to purge Ding as Hitler or Mussolini would have done, but instead he made him chairman of a commission to conserve wild life!

After that election I began to take a more hopeful view of things. As long as people are free to criticize their government when they disagree with it, or change it when it doesn't accomplish what they expect of it, no trouble can really be so bad. I quit complaining about my business difficulties and began to thank God that I was a citizen of a land where all these miraculous things could happen as if they were the most ordinary occurrences in the world.

CHAPTER XVII

Paris Round Table

In the spring of 1933, the year that Hitler became Chancellor of Germany, I made a sudden decision to return to Syria to visit the scenes of my boyhood and renew old acquaintances. I wrote to a steamship line, offering to conduct a touring party through the Holy Land in return for the usual fee. To my surprise, they accepted, and I became a guide for a party of students from various colleges and universities who wanted to "do" Egypt and Palestine.

Since my services as guide did not begin until the party reached Beirut, I left early so as to have a few days in Europe. I sailed third-class on the *Olympic*, landed at Cherbourg, and arrived in Paris on the 30th of June. My first interest was to see the usual sights—the Arc de Triomphe, the Invalides, Eiffel Tower, Versailles, the Tuileries, the Louvre, etc. I asked an English acquaintance about guide service, and he introduced me to an affable young French-man by the name of Jacques Pierre. Our conversation after the introduction went something like this:

Surveying me from head to foot with a slow and smiling eye, he said, "You are not one of ze American bankers, are you, Mr. Reesk?"

"No, I'm not," I replied, feeling more than a little flattered by the compliment.

"Are you perhaps zen one of ze American gangsters?" he inquired.

"No, I am not," I said, laughing, although I suppose I should have felt insulted, and would have, had it not been for the mischievous twinkle in his eyes.

"Tell me, Mr. Reesk," he said, the twinkle deepening, "why do you not have in America a gangsters' holiday?"

"A gangsters' holiday? What do you mean?"

"Well, you did have ze bankers' holiday—one day the bankers couldn't rob anybody. You should have a gangsters' holiday, too—one day when ze gangsters don't shoot anybody."

The mischief in Jacques's eyes told me that I was going to have a good time with him, and a revealing one, too. He was well informed about America, although not always very accurately, because he believed too many head-lines, and he was frank and had a delightful sense of humor.

"America is not just a place for bad bankers and gangsters," I said.

"Who zen is ruining America? Somebody has to ruin it."

"America isn't being ruined. It is just suffering from the same depression you have here in France."

"Here in France we only have ze bankers to ruin us," he persisted. "Maybe we will survive. But how can any country survive two plagues at once?"

"America has survived the worst plague of all, a civil war, so I don't think she'll have any trouble getting over any lesser plagues."

"Mon Dieu, Monsieur Reesk," he cried, "do you not almost have civil war in America now? If it is as bad as ze papers say, it is very, very bad."

"What do your French papers say?"

"Zey say people are starving by the millions. The Army is called out every day to crush revolts. They put down the bonus marchers and the hunger marchers in ze capital. Ze farmers lose their fields, the workingmen freeze in ze bread lines, ze rich run over ze poor and unemployed workers in the streets, and ze workers make revolt in the cities. It is very bad, what we hear. Pretty soon America have the revolution, yes?"

"Oh no, my friend, things are not that bad. Your papers exaggerate if they give you that impression. Sure, we have hard times. Many people are hungry and dissatisfied, but I don't think anybody is seriously thinking of overthrowing the government."

"Ah yes, but when people are hungry, then they want a Mussolini or a Hitler, or maybe a Stalin. Your President, this Mr. Roosevelt, is he not himself a revolutionist? Will he not drive ze moneymakers from ze temple?"

"He said he would, and I think he will. But that is not revolution, unless it is a revolution at the polls. The people voted for a New Deal and——"

"Maybe what zey need is a new deck. Mr. Reesk, tomorrow night I go to a club meeting at the Y.M.C.A. Everybody come from different country. We are what you call mix-up—English, Italian, German, Swiss, Dutch, Czech, everything. You come with me, yes? Tomorrow at eight."

As Jacques had said, the meeting was "mix-up"; a score of nationalities were represented by the young men gathered there. They were eager to learn about America, and as soon as introductions were over they began to ply me with personal questions.

"What is your profession in America, Mr. Reesk?" a French student asked.

"I have no profession," I replied. "I am a shoemaker."

"Ah, a shoe manufacturer."

"No sir. I am a shoe repairer, a shoe cobbler." They laughed; they thought I was fooling. One of them said, "Perhaps, then, Monsieur does not wish to tell us what he——"

"Pardon, but I am not joking," I said. "That is my trade. I am a shoemaker."

"But, monsieur, you a shoemaker, and you dress like this, and you travel in Europe! And you are educated! Where can you find a shoemaker like that?"

"In America you can find them."

I had to explain that I did not carry a little box of tools, as the European shoemakers did, and trudge from house to house, begging for business. I told them about my shop, equipped with hundreds of dollars' worth of modern machinery, and how I paid big rent—sixty-five dollars a month —and employed several people to work with me.

They could hardly believe it. One of them said mockingly, "Now you will tell us that a shoemaker owns and drives his own private car."

"Sure," I said, "I drive my own car. I have had three cars since I have been in America."

"Three cars since you have been in America! How long have you been there?"

"Six years."

"Monsieur, how can that be! It is impossible to believe. I have lived in France all my life and have never owned even one car. Where were you before you went to America?"

"I lived in Syria."

"Mon Dieu, it is getting worse. You are from Syria, a French colony, and you go to America an immigrant and you are better off than a Frenchman who lives all his life in France?"

I had to admit it, even if it did hurt his pride. And so the conversation went, probing deeper and deeper into America. I tried to keep to the common things, and the common people, of America, to the things that never get into distorting headlines, to the comforts and well-being enjoyed by great masses of people in spite of the depression—ice boxes, refrigerators, telephones, radios—things as common as cabbage in our homes. I began to think perhaps I was painting the picture too bright. At any rate a Pole opened up on me and said, "All you Americans can think of is money, money, money. You measure everything with money. Is it not your expression, 'Bring home the bacon'? You think your country is a piece of bacon, a banquet table from which to feast. But we Poles think of our country as an altar—an altar upon which to sacrifice ourselves and all our possessions."

"Unfortunately," I said, "you know that is not altogether true of either Poles or Americans. We have both kinds of people in all countries. You have Poles who think of their country only as a banquet table, too, and we have Americans who look on their country as an altar."

"I say," said a tall, dissipated Englishman in baggy clothes, "sometimes I think—indeed, I am convinced—that you Americans regard the whole world as your banquet table."

"Perhaps," said a meek-looking little Hindu, "it might be well to remind the British that India is somebody's banquet table, too."

"Yes, it is true, all you have said," cried a dark little fellow, leaping to his feet and making his face fierce. "You all think of life as a banquet table. All you want to know is, 'What can I get?' Do you know the answer to that? Have you found it in America, in France, in England? No. But we have found it. We have found it in Italy. Il Duce has found it. Il Duce is the answer. Il Duce has put an end to greed and grabbing. Now we have peace. We have order. We have decency.

"Before he rose to save our nation," he continued, referring to Mussolini, "Italia was not fit to live in. We had the Mafia, who were even worse than the gangsters in America, and the Communists, who were worse than the Mafia, and a government that was worse than either of them. A government that was so helpless, inefficient, and full of corruption that, when the Communists took over the factories and railroads, it could do nothing. There was a general revolt, strikes everywhere. The whole industry of Italy was at a standstill. And while all was chaos, there was bitter poverty, squeezing us into despair. Then came Il Duce, and with his strong will and ability as a statesman he restored order, established law, compelled obedience, and made our nation great again. Instead of the greedy, plutocratic owners and the duped workers and Communists, we have the Fascist state. We have authority and efficiency. We have strength and glory. Italy again is great."

At that instant another young man, a dark, stocky fellow, with pudgy features and thick, black eyebrows, leaped to his feet. I learned later that his father had been killed by the Fascists, and that he escaped from Italy and was now working as a mechanic in an American car agency in Paris. He spoke with fierce conviction. "Yes, Italy has authority and efficiency, but not strength and glory. Don't forget, signor, you are not speaking to little children eager to swallow everything the Fascist catechism misleads you to believe. You believe Mussolini made order in Italy. You say the troubles in Italy were caused by war and Communists and Socialists. But who converted the people to socialism with his eloquent speeches and editorials? Who ranted against the plutocrats and bloody exploiters, the profiteers and warmongers? Who taught the workers to revolt and take over the plants and create confusion? Who finally exhorted his followers to join the war on the side of the Allies? If you do not know, since your Fascist catechism does not tell you, I will point him out. It is your great Il Duce! the traitor, the misleader, the opportunist who betrayed his people for his own advantage, who murdered and is still murdering his best friends and former comrades in socialism to win power and inflate his own ego.

"What good is efficiency if it degrades men and makes them all groveling slaves of the corporate state? What good is it to wipe out the Black Hand from Italy only to put the heavy foot of Fascism on its neck?

"Once Mussolini promised to be a great leader, a leader of the workers, a leader of the people, but when he traded his soapbox for the Palazzo Venezia, he became a howling beast, a hyena."

It was the most impassioned speech I had ever heard When the little Italian sat down, the tension in the room was terrific. I wondered what would happen next. A young man from Switzerland spoke: "I am told that once Benito Mussolini was speaking from the Palazzo Venezia, telling his people of all the great and glorious things he had done for Italy, when a man in the audience muttered, 'Yes, but if we had half as much to eat as we have to swallow, it would be even greater and more glorious.' "

We laughed—all except the fiery little Fascist. His face was contorted with bitter rage. The Italian Socialist turned to him and said, "Laugh, my friend, laugh. Remember you're not in Italy now. You are in a free place where people still laugh at jokes instead of saluting them."

That was too much for the Fascist. Shouting what I gathered to be Italian expletives of the lowest order, he stomped angrily from the room.

The rest of the evening we spent arguing about Europe —history, politics, economics, religion. At one point, overwhelmed by the confusion of problems, I turned to the Englishman beside me and said, "Poor Europe. I wish the peoples here could be as peaceful and friendly as those same people are when they get to America."

The Englishman lifted his brows. "You Americans are very smug," he said. "You believe yourselves to be immune from the diseases which afflict us. But don't forget that someday America will wake up to find herself in the same mess as Europe. You know, Macaulay once said that the chief difference between the United States and Europe is that your country is always about sixty years behind us —and that goes for the evil in us as well as the good."

Afterward Jacques and I and three or four others went to a café and sat up until four o'clock in the morning, still talking European politics and American life. They were much more interested in the latter and kept me busy answering a thousand and one questions about our thoughts and ways. My friends listened like little children, their eyes filled with wonder. You could see that every one of them was wishing in his inmost heart that he might go to my country and live there forever. Yes, Jacques even said jokingly, though I think there was a wistfulness in it, too, "Maybe I am an American just as you were and don't know it. Maybe we are all Americans." . . . In a deeper sense I felt he was right. . . .

So when I fell asleep that morning, blissfully tired, no one can blame me for feeling like a king. I awoke later that same morning, though, feeling like something a good deal less than a king. In the Paris headlines I learned I had been robbed: President Roosevelt had devalued the dollar. My money was now worth only half as much. The President's move had been forced by the European situation. An anxious thought crossed my mind: Maybe the Englishman was right—more right than he knew. Maybe someday America *would* find herself in the same mess as Europe.

CHAPTER XVIII

To Beirut via Italy

IT HAD BEEN MY PLAN to go to Germany next, but my friends dissuaded me. "Keep your nose out of Germany," they said. "It looks too Jewish." So I did not go to Germany, but in a most unexpected way I got to see it anyway. Really I think I got a better picture of inside Nazi Germany and all its awful, sadistic cruelty than if I had been on a guided, or perhaps I should say a misguided, tour through Hitler's new national prison house.

But before that I saw Italy. At the border two officials examined my baggage. They found a suspicious-looking book entitled, *Synonyms and Antonyms.*

"Who are they?" one of them asked.

"Who are who?"

"They, they!" he said, pointing excitedly at the title.

"Oh, they," I said. "They're a couple of revolutionists."

"R-r-r-evolushionists!"

"Sure, revolutionists."

"You are under arrest."

"Don't be foolish," I said, reaching for the book.

But he was serious. Before I was extricated from that spot I had to talk to a higher-up. Never again will I travel in a Fascist country without knowing the antonym for "revolutionist."

In Trieste I went sight-seeing with an Italian from Brooklyn and a Jewish professor from Boston University, both of whom I had met on the *Olympic* coming over. At the seashore we were amazed at the large number of soldiers and sailors strolling up and down, sitting idly on benches, or making love to dark-eyed young women. The men in uniform looked happy, well fed, and satisfied—a striking contrast to the hungry, ragged, barefooted people we had seen peddling wares from pushcarts and trays on the streets back in the city.

The Boston professor tossed his head in the direction of the soldiers. "This is the way Mussolini solves his unemployment problem," he said.

"How do you mean?"

"When a man loses his job, he puts him in a uniform—makes a soldier out of him."

"What a terrible solution!" I said. "Is that the best that Fascism can do—hide its problems behind a military glamour?"

"No, it does even better with the women. There are no unemployed women in Italy, either. All of them are busy raising babies for the State—for the conquering armies of Rome. They've all been ordered to quit work and get husbands."

"Don't the men have anything to say about it?"

"Not much. To make the men willing, the government has clamped on a stiff bachelor's tax. Then, to make it easy for a couple to raise a family, they give a bonus for every baby. Anyway, that's what it amounts to. When a couple get married, they get a government loan. When they have four children, the loan is canceled. Then the government takes the babies and trains them for military service. It's the greatest system yet devised for conquering the world. Works automatically. Just like a slot machine. Put in a loan, take out four babies. Put in four babies, take out four soldiers. Put in four soldiers, take out a new colony. If the Roman Empire doesn't go places under this system, it won't be Mussolini's fault."

"It'll be his fault," I said, "if he raises more people than he can feed."

"In that case, you just stir up a war and get the surplus killed off."

"My God," I exclaimed, "what kind of madness is this!"

"It's a madness that's hard to describe. . . . Do you remember the experience Smedley Butler had with Mussolini here some months ago?"

"You mean the time Mussolini was showing Butler around, and he hit a child with his car?"

"Yes. Do you recall what Mussolini said when Butler asked him if he wasn't going to stop and take the child to a hospital?"

"Yes, I remember that. He said, 'What's a child in the affairs of state?' "

"Well, there you have it in a nutshell. That's the kind of madness this is. It's the madness of men with an insatiable lust for power. In a system like this, people don't count. It's the State that counts, and the almighty superman who controls the State."

My time being up in Italy, I booked passage from Trieste to Syria on the *Martha Washington*. I expected it to be a good American ship, but it turned out to be a Fascist boat in the ugliest sense of the word.

I had been told, when buying my ticket, to be at the port exactly at nine or expect to get left, and knowing Mussolini's reputation for promptness I arrived forty minutes early; already it seemed that most of the passengers had gathered. They were a poor, ragged, unkempt-looking lot, and here and there I noticed a bandaged head or face, an arm in a sling, or a body swinging between crutches. Somewhere there had been a delay, so the gangplank didn't come down until ten o'clock. It was fully four hours before I reached the deck and nearly suppertime before my ticket was stamped and a cabin assigned to me.

In my cabin were six bunks, three along each wall, with a narrow aisle for dressing down the middle. I had one of the bunks near the ceiling. Five Jewish immigrants occupied the others. They were old men, bewhiskered and pale, almost sickly, I would say, and very religious. They prayed or read aloud from the Torah practically all hours of the day and half the night. Since religious scruples prevented them from eating the unblessed (in more ways than one) stuff the ship's cook tried to feed us, they had brought their own provisions. The overcrowded cabin soon smelled gloriously of garlic and other vivid victuals, which I was invited to share and which I gratefully accepted as a welcome relief from the Fascist spaghetti.

At first it made me furious to be crowded onto a ship with all this disabled, pushing, crowding, sweating humanity, and with such poor facilities, bad food, and worse service, not to mention the plug-ugly pictures of the Italian dictator which domineered the decks and passageways from every wall. The thought crossed my mind that the ship might have been more appropriately christened *Benito Mussolini*.

For a while I didn't know what to do with myself. The

cabin was too crowded, noisy, and stuffy to read in. I didn't know anyone to talk to; everybody spoke in a foreign language. I had lost track of my professor friend from Boston and couldn't remember his name to ask for him at the registry. The decks were overflowing with humanity day and night. Many of the passengers were stretched out in sheer exhaustion right on the deck, so that you were always walking over or around crumpled bodies, and over the whole scene was a constant excited babble and tumult of voices. I began to chide myself for not investigating the boat before booking passage.

Finding an empty deck chair, I sat down and idly surveyed the crowded litter of humanity on the deck. Then a feeling of guilt came over me. My mind had been busy with my own inconvenience and discomfort. Six years earlier, when I crossed the Atlantic the first time, I would have thought a boat like this quite magnificent. What had happened to me? Had I grown soft, pampered, self-indulgent, self-centered? For the first time I really saw the people on the boat, saw them as they were, as separate persons, and wondered about them. Men and women with heads and faces wrapped in bandages. Why? Arms in slings, legs in casts.

There was a man who limped, every step stabbing pain into his eyes and face; another man—and there were others like him—sprawled on the deck who moaned and groaned when he moved; and others who lifted their voices in a kind of wailing when they talked

That evening I happened into a meeting on board the ship. There I found my Boston professor friend. His face was flushed with excitement. Agitation was in his eyes and face and hands.

"What's the meeting about?" I asked him.

"That's a long story, Rizk," he said. "This meeting is of the *Chalutizim*—the Young Pioneers' Society. They're mostly all Jews headed for Palestine."

"Where do they all come from?"

"Ah, that's the sad part of it. They're running away, Rizk, running away from home, the only home they've ever known. All their lives they've lived in Germany, good, patriotic citizens, most of them thrifty, honest, industrious, middle-class people. Now they're running away from the Nazi terror."

"The Nazi terror! You mean the Nazis have done this to them?" I had read something about that in the newspapers, but had never imagined I would see a whole shipload of the flesh-and-blood victims of this latest edition of tyranny. And how much worse it is when you see it with your own eyes than when you read about it!

"Yes, and more," the professor said, answering me. "A lot has happened to them that you can't see on their faces or bodies. I've been listening to their stories all morning.

You should hear them. It sounds like something out of the Dark Ages. Whippings, beatings, boycotts, cruelties, tortures, and indignities of the vilest kind. It started with ostracism—children barred from the schools, streets, and playgrounds; professional men barred from the libraries; every Jew denied use of the parks, their shops and offices painted up, picketed, and raided by Nazi hoodlums. Behind every one of these busted heads, smashed noses, broken jaws and limbs is a story of long hours and days of inward agony and physical torture. Some of these people have been hung by their heels, head down, for hours at a time and whipped or cut and jabbed with knives, until they fainted from pain and loss of blood. Some of the men were herded into sties and made to crawl on their hands and knees and squeal like pigs while guards lacerated their buttocks with long, sharp whips; or for variation they were forced to beat each other up. But it's what they try to do to the spirit of a people that makes the real hurt. When a man is afraid and ashamed of his blood and birth, when he cries to God to take the curse of his race from off his back—that's the real tragedy, that's what hurts."

"My God!" I exclaimed. "What sort of men are these Nazis?"

"They're not men, Rizk. They're beasts." A kind of pain —the pain of vicarious fear—flashed over his face.

"Why, these people are lucky to be alive," I said.

"I don't know. Sometimes I think they'd be better off dead. They've lost everything—everything accumulated in a lifetime wiped out in a few hours or days—businesses, homes, money, securities; absolutely stripped. And their families have been scattered to the four winds. They may never see each other again. Their whole world has gone to pieces, smashed in an instant by the orders of a ruthless tyrant. But they think they can pick up the pieces in Palestine."

"But why do they want to go to Palestine? There's nothing for them there—no opportunities, no resources, no anything."

"There's the only hopeful thing about this whole business. These people don't need opportunities. They make opportunities. That's what the meeting's about tonight. They're getting the lay of the land and perfecting their organization. They have some brilliant young leaders, men educated in Europe's finest schools. They are full of fire, full of hopes, ideas, plans. And what's more, they know how to work."

"But if they've lost everything, what are they going to work with? After all, they have to have tools and things."

"They have. They have each other to work with. That's what one of them told me this afternoon. And, you know, it occurred to me since then that that is the most beautiful and efficient and powerful tool under the sun. That's what's so exciting about the whole thing. You ought to hear them talk. No idle patter, no criticism, no bickering. Their talk is like a man walking upstairs. Every time one of them says something, it carries the whole group a little higher, another step forward—the most constructive talk I've ever heard. And everything is just like that—down-to-earth mutual-aid idealism. Necessity, more than anything else, forces them to it. They've got to pool their brains and energies if they want to survive."

The professor's face shone with an enthusiasm that was beautiful. My own interest was deeply kindled. "I wish I could understand what they're talking about."

"Don't worry," he said. "After the meeting I'll tell you about it."

And he did—and a lot more besides. He told me of their marvelous plans to rebuild their broken life—homes to build, soil to till, food, water, and medicine to provide, shoes, stockings, clothes, furniture, schools, till I doubted they could do it all, starting with practically nothing. But when he told me of the already established communities, like the village of Ain Harod in the plain of Esdraelon, a new Jewish colony, where the people owned their own bakery, clothing factory, canning and brick plant, I could no longer doubt. I could only stand in awe of the tough human stuff that could come back in the face of such complete disaster and build again all that solid, peaceful life that was lost. "There's an old saying," the professor said, "that the bee fertilizes the flower which it robs. No race has been robbed so much as the Jews, and no race has given so much to mankind. Perhaps, by robbing and bruising these people, the dictator has only added the creative ingredient that will bring new fruit from their talents and energies. By the same token the tyrant has perhaps sown the seeds which will encompass his own destruction."

When, some days later, the bruised and wounded people, with all their possessions tied up in sacks and bags, left the ship, I went to my cabin and wrote in my diary:

I am ashamed. When I left Syria for America, I was going from a poor, stricken land to the richest, freest, mightiest country on earth—and I was afraid, afraid I wouldn't be able to make it, afraid I couldn't fit in. But these people, uprooted and exiled from their native soil, where they had life on easy terms, are going to a pale, tired land where life will be hard, where they will have to struggle from the bottom up, where they will have to fight and rustle every minute to wrest a few crumbs of existence from stingy Nature, and where they will face the suspicion and hostility of their constantly agitated Arabic neighbors—and they are not afraid. They are brave, inspired, and determined. Since first hearing about it, I have always thought of the resettlement of Palestine as a nice way of disposing of the Jewish problem—creating a national home for these long-wandering exiles of the earth. Now I see in it a hint of an international hope—a way out for democracy and humanity. Perhaps these exiles, detoured from a settled destiny by the dictator's whim, will find their way home by another road—and in the process erect some signposts for the rest of us to follow. They did it before; they will probably do it again.

CHAPTER XIX

Welcome in Ain Arab

WHEN I BEHELD THE HARBOR of Beirut over the ship's prow, I don't know what was the matter, but I couldn't get myself to respond the way I had expected to. One of my friends in America had told me how he had returned to Syria after a long sojourn in Australia and how he had laid a tender, passionate kiss on the stone wall which surrounded his old home in the Lebanon. So I had imagined that the first sight of my homeland would send me into uncontrollable raptures. Instead, I felt foolish. Other Syrian-Americans on the boat shouted blissfully, ecstatically, until they were hoarse, but I was as cold as a fish. Don't think I didn't try to overcome my apathy. I tried hard to make my heart beat faster, tried to feel, "This is my own, my native land." But it was no use. I thought maybe I was abnormal or that Europe had cankered my sense of joy. Or maybe this wasn't the place. Maybe Ain Arab was the place. I would wait and see.

My first impression of Beirut was that it had shrunk terribly. The buildings which had once seemed so tall, the shops, stores, and public buildings which had looked so large and prosperous, the Grand Hotel Victoria which had been so magnificent, all now had become small and modest, almost poor and shabby by contrast with America. This impression struck me even more forcibly in Ain Arab. As I approached the village, in a Model T taxi, it looked like a lifeless skeleton bleaching in the desert.

But before we reached Ain Arab a funny thing happened. From the main highway between Beirut and Damascus a new, narrow-lane road leads through the thin, scraggly country to my village. Because of the loose gravel, which sent nervous shivers through every seam and joint of the ancient vehicle I had hired and because of the sharp curves which swept suddenly around the hills, our average speed could not have been over ten miles an hour. What slowed us up, too, was that we had to stop now and then to drive donkeys, goats, or camels from the road. But, worst of all, my driver was a Moslem. At one point he stopped the car and, in the absence of water, performed his ablutions by washing in the red soil of an adjacent field, and then, spreading his prayer rug, knelt toward Mecca and began, *"Allah akbar! Ashhadu en la illah illa allah . . ."*

It was his hour of prayer. I sat in the car and waited. The intoning went on and on—about twenty minutes of it. At first I was impatient and was about to interrupt him to plead for a postponement, when, looking about, I saw perhaps a dozen other figures, shepherds and fellaheen in the fields and pastures, all fallen in the same attitude of reverence and devotion. I could not disturb them. So presently I amused myself trying to picture a Moslem America. I saw fast trains coming to a stop out in the country, after which the engineer leaped from his cab and spread his rug on the right of way, followed by all the Mohammedan members of the crew and all the Mohammedan passengers. I imagined taxi drivers on Fifth Avenue suddenly halting their cars and hitting the pavement, and street-car conductors, bus drivers, street cleaners, bootblacks, doctors, merchants, and public officials. I saw golfers kneeling on greens and fairways, and policemen interrupting the pursuit of a criminal to keep the faith. I saw workers on an automobile assembly line let a car go through without a carburetor or minus a fender in order to keep their tryst with Mecca. It was an intriguing interlude. Presently the Moslem finished his prayers, picked up his rug, and climbed into the car. His face was filled with an indescribable serenity and peace. I wouldn't have robbed him of that bliss for anything.

Not until we drove into the middle of the town—the town where I was born and spent my boyhood—did I feel anything of the thrill which I had anticipated for so long.

Someone shouted, "Salom is here. Salom has come." The sound of my name shouted in that place brought tears to my eyes. Suddenly the car was surrounded with people. I leaped over the door of the back seat, and the men and older women fell upon me, shouting and crying and kissing me with a hundred kisses and stirring up enough dust to choke an army. Then my grandmother Gontoosy broke into a song of welcome, piling up all the glorious phrases of gratitude and hospitality which always make me glad I was born a Syrian. This was the real thing. Maybe I was normal after all. But it was the people and not the place that made me feel that way.

That night there was a great gathering of people at my grandmother's house which I shall never forget as long as I live. Almost everybody in the village was there, either crowded into the house or milling around outside, waiting for a chance to squeeze in. There was Tuma, the village shoemaker and kindly cynic, who had been a peddler in Mexico, where exposure to communism had filled him with contempt for religion, and who had won such a wide following among the simple people of the church that the priest had to ask him to lay off. The priest was there too, fat, jolly, and careless, a very ordinary man, whose job was to perform rituals and bawl the people out for not attending them. There was Abu Nimur, a returned immigrant, who had gotten half the village into his debt by lending the people money at exorbitant interest from his American-made fortune; with subsequent foreclosures on fields and vineyards, he had become the wealthiest individual in the village—and the most hated. And then there was old Hanan, hard and vital and bitter—bitter because he had left America (that paradise of all the earth, he called it) without becoming a citizen and had never been able to return. They said that in crazy moments he beat his head with a hammer and cursed the devils within which had tempted him back to Syria.

Yes, poor old Hanan. He looked so lost and pathetic sitting there in the dim light of the sputtering candles and the kerosene lamp . . . the long, shadowed lines that pulled his dark, leathery face down . . . and the eager light that lit his eyes when something I said stirred old memories.

"I curse every hour that I live for ever coming back," he said.

"You must not feel too bad, Hanan," I said, trying to think of something to console him. "In some ways you are many times better off than in America. We have a depression in America. Millions of people are out of work. And when you are out of work in America, you are desperate. Without work you cannot get money, and without money you cannot buy food, or water, or warmth, or clothing, or anything else. You are a beggar and have to take alms from the rich or from the state. Here it is different. You may be poor, but you are not a beggar. You have the land and the wood in the hills and all the wild things. You have the water from the common well, and the water mills to grind your grain. Many people in America wish now they had as much."

"Yes, but America is better, America is better," he moaned. "Besides, things are getting worse here, much worse, since the French came."

"Yes, yes," said Tuma, explaining with his wider understanding, "that is the truth. The French have tied us to the world market, and now we are just like the American farmer—low prices for what we sell and high prices for what we buy."

"How did they do that—I mean, tie you to the world market?"

"With their damnable taxes. They make us pay taxes in money. To get money we have to take our grain to the city, and in the city we take what they give us."

"Then you think you were really better off under the Turks?"

"In some ways," said Asaad, who was one of the more prosperous fellaheen. "The Turks couldn't think of so many ways to tax us. The French think of nothing but taxes. Just think of it, we have to pay a tax on schoolbooks."

"And on dogs, too," said Nagaeeb.

"And on legal notes," added Asaad. "You can't even borrow money on your word of honor any more. It isn't legal. You have to write it on a paper and paste a French stamp on it."

"Yes," said Nagaeeb, shaking his fist in the face of an imaginary Frenchman, "and they send us tax bills, too, and collect in cash. The Turks never did that. They just came and took what they wanted and went away. Now to get money we have to put our wheat on a donkey and go clear to Damascus."

Everybody laughed at that because Damascus, twenty-five miles away, represented the uttermost limits of travel in this part of Syria.

"You don't have to use a donkey now," said Asaad. "You can take wheat to Damascus cheaper by truck. That's what I've been trying to tell you. If we all go together we can hire a truck——"

"Ach, a truck," snorted Nicola, "a truck, when we have donkeys! You want us to feed the donkeys and make them lazy in the pasture. Do you think my donkey is better than I am that he should eat and not work?"

"Figure it out, Nicola," Asaad said. "You will find that one truck will carry more wheat than all the donkeys in Ain Arab, and do it ten times faster. Do you think people get rich in America hauling grain to market on a donkey?"

Asaad looked at me as if for confirmation.

"I have been thinking," I said, "of how much of America

has come to Syria, and how much more of it would come if you would let it, if you would help it. Fords, Chevrolets, motion pictures, telephones, radios, all from America. I saw them in Beirut. You might even have them here in Ain Arab."

"Not with the French here," said Asad. "They milk us with both hands and complain because there is not more."

"Surely, Asaad," I said, "the French government gives you something for your taxes."

"Gives us something?" he said, puzzled.

"Yes, renders you some service."

"The government renders us service?"

I suddenly saw that the question seemed foolish to him. I was talking to a man born and bred in another tradition— the tradition I had been spending six years forgetting—the tradition under which a government is a vast, capricious, overhead monopoly of violence and greed and crime, something unamenable, like the weather, sometimes kind and sometimes cruel, but always to be feared just because it is there.

"In America the government gives us services for our taxes, because the government really belongs to us, to the people," I explained. "We tell it what to do, and it does it —sometimes."

"Ya, ya," said Asaad. "Your government is upside down.

and was going to return the next day. I asked him to buy me a bunch of grapes, ripe grapes. I could pin them on my grandmother's vines and hasten my departure.

But Michael brought the wrong kind of grapes. So I just said I was going; I might miss my boat. I could not leave Ain Arab, though, without weeping. "Please take me with you," they cried. "Put me in your pocket. . . . Put me in your suitcase. . . . Let me be your servant. . . . Buy me a ticket." And when I assured them that all that was impossible, they begged and pleaded with me to use my power, my influence, and the influence of my friends to get them into America.

"Step on the gas, Michael," I said. "They're breaking my heart."

And I meant it. They really were.

CHAPTER XX

"Lend Me Your Ears"

BACK IN THE UNITED STATES AGAIN, I was assailed with an overmastering urge to get my feelings about this European experience off my chest. I wanted to seize people, buttonhole them on the street, tell them what wonderful things we had here: peace, plenty, tolerance, freedom, friendliness, opportunity, genuine human happiness—the greatest, the most beautiful, the most miraculous things on earth.

I wanted to tell them to hang onto them, to increase and multiply them, to give them to the rest of the world, to shout them from the mountains and the prairies, the skyscrapers, the cathedral spires and radio towers.

I wanted to tell them how much we needed to roll up our sleeves and go to work with new zeal to lick our problems, to lick poverty, prejudice, ignorance, injustice, to lick greed, hate, corruption, rackets, to lick every evil in ourselves and outside ourselves that stood between the American people and the great American dream.

I wanted to tell them that we, the people, weren't licked as long as we kept faith with our dream and saw our problems, not as plagues, but as challenges, as opportunities.

I wanted to tell them that if we did as much for America as America has done for us, we need never worry about the outcome, no matter how long and hard the road. Yes, there were so many things I wanted to say then and now, I don't have room to record them all.

Two things I now knew had happened to me since sailing from America. First, I had a new love of her that made all my previous feelings seem thin, shallow, unreal. Now I loved her intemperately, with a fresh and violent infatuation such as lovers feel after a long separation. It seemed that I loved her more physically now, and, because more physically, more spiritually, too. As the swift train sped me homeward through the fair and teeming countryside, every detail of America's life struck my eyes with a fresh force and a fresh wonder, highlighted by the dark afflictions of the Old World. It was as if every hill and valley, every field and tree and stone, every chimney, steeple, and spire, every smokestack and every water tower shone with an inward light. Liberty, peace, well-being lay like a radiance on the landscape, a part of it, the cause of it, the things that have made America what it is. Even the begrimed and sooted cities, with their ghostlike factories, closed by a calamitous depression, glowed with the promise of better days. Bad as things were here, I knew they were infinitely better than in Europe or, for that matter, anywhere else in the world.

I can't say that these feelings were precisely patriotic, at least not in any ordinary sense, for I had an overwhelming wish that the whole world might share in all of it; that the kindly, poverty-stricken people I had so recently visited in Syria, and who had yearned, even begged, so pathetically for passage to America, might have a land like this to live in; that the Jewish exiles returning to the lean and stony ridges of Palestine might have found resources as rich as these, an air to breathe as free of hate and fear as this, and a welcome—yes, a welcome as warm and rousing as the words inscribed to the huddled masses of the Old World on our own Statue of Liberty.

Secondly, if I was aware of loving America with a new heart now, I was also aware of seeing her with new eyes; I was more critical of her; more critical because more concerned. And concerned, not about myself only, but about her—my country's—safety and destiny. I remembered the Englishman in Paris quoting Macaulay, saying that the chief difference between the United States and Europe was that the United States was always about sixty years behind developments in the Old World, implying that eventually we too would be driven to the same good or evil solutions. Macaulay had said that before life had speeded up. The time was surely shorter now. It might be only ten years now, or five or three. That was a thought to haunt the mind. In Europe I had heard men tell how vicious demagogues exploited desperate people to lift themselves to power. I had heard and seen how dictators had organized hatred and intolerance into ruthless machines of violence and destruction, converted the unemployed masses into huge armies, and trampled the most sacred rights and values of free men underfoot. There was soil in America for the same sort of deadliness to take root: racial prejudice, poverty, unemployment, discontent, despair of democracy. Even before going to Europe I had sometimes felt uneasy at reactions I encountered. Mussolini's brags about Fascismo solving poverty had found welcome lodging in certain American ears. Hitler's maltreatment of the Jews appealed to some of my friends as good common sense. There were those, especially disillusioned young people, who applauded Stalin's arbitrary arrests, killings, and starvation as the future liberation of humanity from the evils of arbitrary arrest, killings, and starvation.

With all the things I had read and knew about America now crystallizing under the impact of what I had seen and heard in Europe, my mind fairly boiled with activity.

Back at work again at my cobbler's bench at the tail end of the summer, I cooled off. There was nobody much to talk to, and my enthusiasm sagged. The college town was dead: it was the lull between summer school and the regular fall term.

With the reopening of school, however, my spirits quickly revived. Here in Ames people were friendly—and alert. Home from their vacations, they dropped in to say hello, learned about my trip to Europe and wanted to hear the story. In a short time invitations to speak here, there, and everywhere came in. Luncheon clubs, college classes, church groups, P.T.A.s—all kept me busy in the most exciting winter I had spent in this country thus far. Even farmers from out in the country asked me to speak to their organizations at little crossroad country schools, the lighthouses of democracy in the frozen hills of this snow-covered Iowa landscape. To those dirt farmers—solid, honest-looking people—I talked about the New Deal coming to their rescue. "In America," I said, "we like to think that we are rugged individualists, and that of all rugged individualists the farmer is the most rugged and self-reliant. Yet look at how much help he gets from the government: weather reports, stock-market reports, agricultural bulletins, extension services, free laboratory tests, pest-eradication services, county agents, soil-erosion control. If the Syrian farmer got one tenth the help the American farmer gets, he would think he was in heaven."

To everybody I talked about the new terror in Europe. My story went just as before, but now I added my observations of the ugly crop of cruelties and oppressions growing in the lands where democracy was dead. I talked about

Hitler's treatment of the Jews, Mussolini's repressive government and fake prosperity, feeding his own people short rations and the rest of the world Fascist baloney. I dealt with some of the worst features of imperialism in Syria and argued with Mussolini about whether war is ennobling or not.

As a diversion, I sometimes used an imitation of Hitler which brought down the house. I would comb my hair down over my forehead with a black pocket comb, then place the comb, mustache-like, over my upper lip, throw my hand up in a brisk Nazi salute, and in a harsh, Hitler-like voice shout, *"Wir dursten nach Rache. Das Blut muss fliesen."* Not very good German, I guess, but then neither is Hitler's. There was also a pugnacious imitation of the Italian dictator strutting on the balcony of the Palazzo Venezia.

That winter I told my story to half the county, it seemed, to its villages and towns and cities—Ames, Nevada, Cambridge, Huxley, Luther, Ogden, Boone, Madrid, Slater, Gilbert, Jordan, Story City, Roland, McCallsburg, Strattford, Stanhope, Des Moines.

Winter over, and speaking opportunities at a standstill, I suffered a recurring restlessness. Repairing shoes irked my spirit. It was a good job as long as I wanted to cobble, but now I wanted to do something else. How was I going to continue telling people my story, the idea that kept pressing to the front of my mind? My friends would come in and say, "Sam, you shouldn't be repairing shoes. You should be out telling your story."

One day a letter came from Iowa City. It was from a friend who had been director of the Congregational Student Center at Ames, and who was now studying medicine at the University of Iowa. His name was Harold Schmidt. The winter before I went to Europe he had invited me to address a religious meeting one Sunday evening. After the meeting, he said, "Sam, you've got a message that every American ought to hear. I'm not fooling when I say that that's the best story I've ever heard, and the most enlightened Americanism to boot."

People had said that sort of thing before—"every American ought to hear you"—schoolmen, college professors, high-school superintendents, bankers, farmers, workers, parents, teachers, students, they'd all said it. But that's as far as it went. And that's as far as I thought this would go. I was mistaken. The next morning Harold called at my shop with an armload of books for me to read and an old pair of shoes to repair. We talked a long time about conditions in America, about things in Europe and my life in Syria. Harold asked a lot of questions. The more I told him about it all, about my discovery of America, my love of its ways and life, my slant on things, the more enthralled he became. Before he left, he said, "Sam, there ought to be some way for you to get your story before more people. It's just the sort of thing a lot of us smug Americans need today. The trouble with most of us is that we were born with our citizenship, which is just about the easiest, cheapest, and worst way to get it. We're inclined to take our opportunities and liberties for granted. We seldom or never stop to think what life would be like without them. But your case is different. You had to earn your citizenship. You were born where all these privileges were denied you. And you know the difference. You have felt the difference in your flesh and bones. You've got to tell the rest of us what it feels like. You can wake us up. Sam, you've got to get America by the ears."

"Hello?" I had said, puzzled. "Get America by the ears? How do you do that?" I had never heard that expression before, and it stopped me.

"You've read Mark Antony's speech, 'Friends, Romans . . . lend me your ears,' haven't you?" Harold asked, laughing.

"No, who's Mark Antony?"

"He's a character in a Shakespearean play. You know who Shakespeare is."

Yes, I knew who he was. I had heard about him in school. Also, I had heard some of my patriotic Syrian-American friends, who were always finding new proofs of the past glory of our race, argue that Shakespeare was not an Englishman at all but a Syrian. The name Shakespeare, they said, was a corruption of his real Arabic name, which was Sheik Esper. They never said how he got to London.

"Mark Antony," Harold went on to say, "is a friend of Julius Caesar's in a play by that name. After Caesar's assassination Mark Antony addresses the Romans and opens his remarks by saying, 'Friends, Romans, countrymen, lend me your ears.' It's a figure of speech, Sam, like 'he won her hand' or 'my heart belongs to you.' When I say you should get America by the ears, I mean find some way to reach more people. Get your story out of Story County."

Well, that night I started to struggle through *Julius Caesar*. That was the worst English I ever read. It was worse than the Bible. After reading for several evenings I came to "Friends, Romans, countrymen, lend me your ears," and I knew what it meant—get out of Story County.

Well, now here was this letter from Harold, inviting me to speak to a church group at Iowa City that spring. Happy to renew this delightful friendship, I went. It was a rural audience I spoke to, and their response was highly pleasing to Harold. After the meeting, we were discussing various things, and I said, "Harold, do you remember Jim Wilson?"

"Do I remember him! How could anybody forget him? He used to teach the seniors in our Sunday school. Nobody ever did a better job. I remember he started out on his lecture tour almost two years ago. He had rigged up a dilapidated old Chevrolet so he could take his family with him, and it was sitting out there on the street in front of the Lincoln apartments. It was just about the most ingenious layout you ever saw. He'd built a cupboard on each fender and one on the rear end to hold practically everything a family needs to live on the road. He had enough stuff on that car to sink the *Leviathan*. I remember how he walked around the darned thing, pointing to the cupboards. 'This one,' he said, 'is the kitchen. This over here is the bedroom, and this one on the rear is the ah—bathroom.' I think he called her Evelyn. Well, tell me, have you heard from Jim lately?"

"I saw him. He stopped in my shop a while back."

"How's he getting along?"

"Great."

"He should. He's got a great story, Jim has—but not any greater than yours, Sam."

"That's what he told me."

"Jim told you that?"

"Yes, he said my story was even better than his, but when I asked him about going out to tell it like he is, he looked dubious. He said it was a tough game, that it was hard to get started when nobody knew you from Adam, and that besides you really had to have something to say and a way of saying it. It really scared me, all the things he said I'd have to know and do."

"Don't let it scare you, Sam. If Jim thinks you've got a good story, then you've got a good story. It's up to us to see that you get a chance to tell it. I'll tell you what you do. You go back to Ames, and when school's out I'll follow. We'll sit down together and work out a plan, make an attractive circular to put in the mail, and then I'll go out on the road and book you."

"Harold, if you'll do that for me I'll be your uncle for life."

"Forget it, Sam," he said. "We'll get along better if we're not related. You run along home now and work on your speech—and remember, your job is to get America by the ears."

I drove back to Ames late that night, across the sleeping countryside, with a Shakespearean chant ringing in my ears: "Friends, Americans, countrymen, lend me your ears. Friends, Americans, countrymen . . ."

CHAPTER XXI

Ups and Downs of Lecturing

"Mr. chairman, ladies and gentlemen, I am not a speechmaker, I am only a shoemaker." That is the way I began my speech back in those days. That is the way I still begin it. I have no illusions about my speaking. I am not a trained public speaker. I have never spent an hour studying anything about how to address an audience. I have a story. The story tells itself—and every time it tells itself I live it over again, every minute of it, really and intensely. That is all there is to it.

But that doesn't mean that lecturing has been easy for me, or that it is easy for anyone. It looks easy. You sit on a platform before an audience of a hundred or maybe a thousand people. The audience looks nonchalant. You look calm. A chairman introduces you. You stand up and give your speech for the thousandth time. You sit down and hear prolonged applause. The chairman closes the meeting, and the audience crowds around you. People shake your hand; they grip it tight. Some of them smile, some laugh, some have tears in their eyes. All are thrilled. They congratulate you. They ask questions. They ask for your autograph. It is all very grand. That's the way it looks. But that isn't the way it is.

You have to begin away back. In the first place, you have a message, or rather, you think you have a message. There are a thousand different ways to tell it. That is the first difficulty. The second one is to find someone to tell it to. And the traveling, the letter writing, the printing and advertising, the mailing and sealing and stamping that it takes just to do that; it's a nightmare. And there is the indifference you meet, and the competition, and the opposition, and the suspicion. Especially the suspicion. People wonder who you are. Are you a foreign agent? Are you a Communist? Are you a fake? What are you up to? Who is behind you? Who is behind the people who are behind you?

Then there is the problem of money. Lecturing means traveling, and traveling means expense—bills, bills, and more bills—gas bills, hotel bills, repair bills, laundry bills, train fares, plane fares. Your message is the first thing. But money—you need so much of it that in spite of every effort to keep it secondary it becomes an important consideration. You can't go five hundred miles to an engagement and talk for nothing. Sometimes you almost wish you were a humble fellah back in Syria who had never heard of lectures and bills and baths and mechanical contraptions or anything else clean and convenient and civilized.

Another thing, you are always away from home. In fact, you have no home. You are a sort of tramp. You live on wheels and out of a suitcase. Every night you sleep in a different room, a different town; every meal you eat in a different café. And your feelings are always wavering between extreme sociability and acute loneliness. One hour you are surrounded with congenial, admiring people, the next hour you eat your heart out in the emptiness of a hotel room or tourist court.

After you get an engagement you have to worry about meeting it. It may rain, or sleet, or snow. Or a tire blows out. Your headlights fail. The car goes on the bum. So you take a bus or you take a plane. Or you drive all night. The next morning you are supposed to deliver a lively lecture.

Then there is the business of getting started. To begin with, you are a nobody. People know you in your own town or your own county, but over in the next county they never heard of you. You get out a map, a big map—of the United States. You look at all the counties in the country; your heart sinks. You have to get all that by the ears. How are you going to do it? You just know you never can.

That's the way I felt when Harold finally arrived in the middle of July 1934 to take over the job of booking me.

The first thing he did was to forget the map of the United States. "We'll start right here at home," he said. "People know you here in Iowa."

But he was mistaken. It is amazing, the number of people who never heard of you. Harold began by writing or talking to people who had heard me speak and asking them for testimonials. Then he went out on the road to arrange my speaking tour. He came back with bad news. The worth-while dates were already filled. Most clubs and organizations which book speakers make their contracts as early as February or March. Now it was August.

Nevertheless we prepared a circular and put it in the mail. The response was feeble. We had sent it to practically all the high schools and churches in Iowa, and there were not more than a dozen replies. We blamed the lateness of our start. We blamed the circular. We blamed my lack of fame. But, of course, that didn't help the bookings.

Two things, however, helped lift our spirits. First, John W. Studebaker, superintendent of the public schools in Des Moines and founder of the first public forums in America, had heard me speak before the Des Moines Rotary Club earlier in the year. Now he asked me to tell my story to the students in the six high schools of his city. Second, Agnes Samuelson, director of public instruction of Iowa, invited me to speak to a state conference of county school superintendents. Following these dates, each of them gave me an encouraging recommendation, which helped a lot. But what helped more was that shortly afterward Mr. Studebaker was appointed by the President to fill the office of Federal commissioner of education. The value of his recommendation suddenly leaped to national importance; Mr. Studebaker's new fame in educational circles made his testimonial good in forty-eight states instead of one. Then, to help still more, Miss Samuelson was elected president of the National Educational Association, giving her recommendation new value outside of Iowa. Harold said, "Sam, you better get down on your knees and start praying for the promotion of everybody who recommends you. The more they succeed, the more you're going to succeed."

As a result of the talk before the county superintendents, I was invited to address fifteen county teachers' institutes in every part of Iowa—Keokuk, Council Bluffs, Maquoketa, Osage, Iowa City, Fort Dodge, Washington, Waterloo, Creston, Red Oak, Jefferson, Oskaloosa. The fees were barely enough to pay expenses. In fact, we had to scrimp like misers to make both ends meet. The back room of my shoeshop was still our headquarters. Most of our meals were bread, milk, and boloney, or Syrian bread and goat cheese from the pantries of my relatives in Sioux City or Cedar Rapids. When we were on the road we slept in the car, shaved in gas-station washrooms, and ate hamburgers and hot dogs. Gasoline and oil we charged, optimistic enough to believe that future bookings would enable us to pay for them.

As the fall season drew to a close, we faced a gloomy prospect. There were only two or three more dates on our calendar, and after that nothing. The last of November, blue and discouraged, we were headed through Missouri for a teachers' institute in southern Illinois. On a bulletin board before a Jewish synagogue in St. Louis we saw announced that Dorothy Thompson was to speak there that evening. We debated whether to stop long enough to hear her. It would mean driving almost all night, but we decided that it would be worth it.

Outside of the fact that Hitler had expelled her from Germany for reporting unpleasant truths about Nazism, I knew little about Dorothy Thompson. Harold knew more. He said she was an ace reporter, with wide experience in Austria and Germany and all that. While we waited he told me about an interesting interview she had had with ex-Chancellor Bruening and how Bruening had envisioned a Europe broken down by the failure of capitalism and overrun by illegitimate gangster governments. He said Hitler made it look as if Bruening might be right.

It was really interesting to watch Harold's mind work as he digested the news and editorials we read together and the speeches we heard. He had read a book called *Decline of the West* by a German named Spengler, and he kept referring to it; prophetic, he said it was. He had a habit of taking the long view of things and trying to dope out their direction. He admitted feeling lost in all the tangle of events, but he said that was no excuse for not trying to figure them out and trying to head them off when they looked evil.

Dorothy Thompson's lecture that night was great, but it was deeply disturbing. She described vividly some of the conditions in Germany that had led to Hitler, and then she told about the Nazis, the beastly things they were doing, the burning of the Reichstag, the pogroms against the Jews, the burning of books and imprisoning of intellectuals. I remember especially the June purges and her story of how the Nazis had killed a certain Willi Schmidt, a music critic, by mistake because he happened to have the same name as another man they were after. That made a deep impression on Harold. Afterwards I said to him, "His last name is the same as yours. That doesn't scare you, does it?"

"No, it doesn't scare me," he said, "but it worries me. Things like that could happen here in America. All you need is a little more hunger, unemployment, and hate. When you think of all the hate for Jews and Negroes and foreigners we have in our own country, it makes you wonder sometimes: what could a clever demagogue and a ruthless party organization do to stir up strife and chaos here? Sometimes I think that one of these days the whole darn world is going to go to pieces at once."

"You're too pessimistic, Harold," I said.

"No, I'm not pessimistic. If I were, I wouldn't be pushing you. Besides, Dorothy Thompson inspired me."

"She did?"

"Why yes, she made me believe more than ever in what we're doing. Sam, just telling your story is going to do a lot to convince Americans to hang onto their heritage, yes, and to improve it, too—if we can get them to listen. But, doggone it, how are you going to do that?"

"I don't know. That's your problem."

"No, it isn't. It's our problem. But we've got to do it." Harold paused, and we drove for a while in silence.

"You know, Sam," he said after some time, "I'll bet some people think I'm queer, concentrating everything on one speaker and one speech, but I keep thinking of what Russell Conwell did with 'Acres of Diamonds,' and I don't care what they think."

So Harold had to tell me about "Acres of Diamonds." "Why don't you write a speech like Conwell's, only make it about America, and then go out and give it yourself?" I told him. "You could probably do much better than I."

"No, I couldn't," Harold said. "You've got one story in a million—yes, in 120,000,000. There just isn't another one like it, and it fits the times like a glove. It really makes people appreciate what it means to live in a country where the government can't shoot Willi Schmidt by mistake."

"Do you think I should tell about Willi Schmidt in my talk?" I asked Harold.

"No, you wouldn't have time for that. Let the Dorothy Thompsons do that. You just keep on telling your own story. We'll get the point."

In spite of this inspiration and Harold's dogged faith and determined labors, lecturing went into a bad slump. Our consequent inactivity plus the American depression and the disturbing news from Europe did strange things to our blood. As a result we got involved in an errant adventure which nearly ended in disaster for both of us. What happened was that we had met a young man who had written a book, the sale of which was to finance a movement to redeem the world. Since we were both ripe for a great deed, young, foolish, idealistic, and worried about the world, we listened to the plan with growing enthusiasm; heard how government people like Mrs. Roosevelt and Henry Wallace, Hollywood people like Will Rogers and Mary Pickford, religious leaders like Muriel Lester and Kagawa, and college presidents like somebody I can't remember, were all interested in the plan. True, the letters from these people did no more than acknowledge receipt of the book and a promise to read it, but it all looked big and important, and our crusading zeal was definitely up.

The plans were really marvelous. First we were to promote the sale of the book, which set the keynote and

sounded the challenge. Then we were to set up a nation-
wide, non-profit, co-operative organization. That much we
actually accomplished. Subsequently, we were to establish
a "Country School" in California to train volunteers in a
technique which borrowed a few pages from the New
Testament, a few more from modern sales methods, and a
few others from an obscure treatise on mass psychology
which the enthusiastic author of the book and of the world
plan had found gathering dust on the shelves of a public
library. After a while we would finance and organize a
traveling university on board a refurbished boat now gathering barnacles on the Eastern seaboard. Then we would
acquire a fleet of airplanes to carry Christianity, medical
service, agricultural advice, and the democratic way of life
to the backward peoples of the earth. One of our number
even interviewed Amelia Earhart on the possibilities of
having her serve as chairman of the air branch.

We began by advertising for representatives in big city
papers all over the country. Since the country was full of
unemployed teachers, executives, bookkeepers, salesmen,
and college graduates, we had no trouble enlisting the
interest of many highly qualified people. They were ready
to become house-to-house agents for the book, ready to
deluge booksellers with beautiful blurbs about it. But we
never got much farther than that. The book was released,
and it was treated rather shabbily by the reviewers. And

then the bills began to come in. The big newspapers which had accepted our ads, the publisher who printed the book, the agents who had been promised allowances—all began to cry for cash. So shortly the whole enterprise folded up.

Harold and I returned to our original job, wiser and poorer by several hundred dollars.

It was midwinter, January 1935, and we were really hard up. Nevertheless, we decided to burn all our bridges behind us. Harold and I each had an old car, and we traded them in on a new one. We had a little ready cash, and we spent it on a new batch of circulars. I disposed of my shoe-shop, and together we went to Chicago, where we had decided to make our headquarters. By picking up a few school and club dates here and there, we managed to hang on until spring, but more than once we were on the verge of surrender.

Once our resources were so low that I had to borrow two dollars from a Japanese restaurant keeper to meet an engagement a hundred miles away. I returned with fifty dollars and gratefully repaid him.

Another time, when we were wondering where next week's room rent was coming from, I was speaking at a public lecture on Chicago's North Side for a percentage of the door receipts. Arriving just before the time for the lecture, I looked into the big auditorium and saw only a handful of people sitting up front. Disappointed, I loitered in the hall, scanning the bulletin boards. Presently three young men came in and stopped in front of a board announcing my program. I overheard one of them say, "I wonder if he's any good." His companions didn't seem to know, so I volunteered, "I've heard this lecture every time it's been given, and I'm going to hear it again." That's all I said. They stepped up to the box office, paid their admission, and went in. . . . Well, after all, it does cost money to get your message around to people.

In Chicago we met many other lecturers, some of whom were experiencing identical difficulties in keeping the wolf at bay. Others, better established and onto the ropes, gave us helpful advice and occasional tips on prospective engagements. Among them were Charles Eagle Plume, a part Blackfoot Indian, who spoke charmingly of the virtues of outdoor life and Indian culture; Van Wormer Walsh, who had a quarter of a million miles of globe-trotting in his traveling bag, and who stumped the country with an excellent repertoire of travelogues on everything from Alaska to Tibet; Bob Morningstar, a dear old fellow, former newspaperman and photographer, who showed pictures and told anecdotes of the great and near-great people he had met; Russell Wright, a nimble-minded young man who had recently returned from an interesting tour of Russia; Slim Williams, the world champion dog-musher, who charmed his audiences with the way he butchered the English language; and Dr. Tarbell, magician and raconteur, the world's foremost practitioner of sightless vision. Never before had I met such an interesting variety of people in such a short time. It was really the best part of a liberal education to rub elbows with them and watch how quickly their minds worked.

One of our new lecture friends told us to ask for a tryout at the annual spring audition of the Chicago Woman's Federation. We did, and it was arranged for me to appear on the same program with Edwin Markham, a thrilling coincidence. I had a few words with the great poet afterwards, but for the life of me I can't remember what he said.

Though the audition brought us a number of engagements for the next fall and winter, we had virtually no bookings and no income to tide us over the summer. After talking it over, we decided that Harold should continue booking, and that I would try to get a job to support both of us. I first tried selling vacuum cleaners; that failed. Then I tried selling curling irons, washing machines, electric mixers, and iceboxes with a crew of salesmen for a big utility company; and that failed. I tried selling a sandwich machine, with no better luck. At last we concluded I couldn't sell anything. Harold wasn't faring much better with my lecture schedule. Much as we hated to admit it, it looked like defeat. I borrowed $400 and bought a shoeshop on the South Side of Chicago. At least I could repair soles. If I lectured at all, it would have to be purely as a side line.

But just when we were ready to acknowledge defeat, circumstances thrust a new challenge into the picture. In a law office in the Chicago Loop, where we had gone to fix up the purchase papers for my shop, we heard something that got us all stirred up again. While an office boy ran over to the courthouse to record the deed, we discussed politics with a Jewish attorney.

"I wouldn't be surprised to see fascism in this country before long," he said.

"What makes you say that?" Harold asked.

"Observation, my friend, observation," the attorney said. "Our firm handles 85 per cent of all the strikes in this area. I know, from dealing with both the companies and the unions on strike cases, that the racketeers who have muscled into the labor unions are ruining them, and I know that the bosses would welcome fascism to clean up the whole mess and put labor in its place."

"What do you mean, the racketeers are ruining the labor unions?" I asked.

"I mean that the present leaders of labor are selling the workingman down the river. They stir up a strike, tell the workers to demand higher wages, shorter hours, better working conditions, anything. So the workers authorize a strike. Then these leaders go to the employers with the bad news. The employers balk, and the racketeers put on the pressure. But before the bosses yield, the racketeers make a proposition. 'Give us $50,000 on the q.t.,' they say, 'and we'll settle the whole thing for you without any more trouble. We'll send the workers back to work, and you can forget the demands.' You see, it's a racket. It could get a throat-hold on the country. That's why a lot of big people would like to see fascism in America."

"Is that a fact!" Harold exclaimed.

"Sure, it's a fact. You don't think I'm spoofing you?"

"No, but it sounds so incredible."

"Believe it or not, that's what we're coming to unless labor cleans house."

"Would you like to see fascism in this country?" Harold asked point-blank.

"Hell, no!" the lawyer exclaimed. "Fascism might begin by hog-tying labor, but it wouldn't stop until it had hog-tied everybody. What some people don't seem to be able to get through their heads is that fascism is just another word for the oldest institution in history—tyranny. And tyranny is one of those things that never goes halfway. It may swallow its victim in pieces, but it never stops until it has swallowed the whole of him. When Mussolini says that the future belongs to fascism, he is only saying what tyrants have always said. And he's not kidding, either."

Riding back to the shop that afternoon, Harold and I discussed the implications of the lawyer's astounding words —big people toying with the idea of fascism right here in America.

"Do you remember that steel worker we met a few weeks ago who said that what this country needed was a dictator to put the Chicago *Tribune* in its place?" Harold asked.

"Yes," I said, "he seemed to think that Roosevelt ought to become what the *Tribune* was accusing him of trying to become."

"Well, that's what makes this whole thing doubly serious. You have people crying for dictatorship from the right because the opposition is abusing its powers, and you have people crying for a dictatorship from the left because their opposition is abusing its privileges."

"You mean, the little tyrants on one side want one big tyrant to take care of all the little tyrants on the other side?"

"That's just about it," Harold said. "Doesn't it make you feel helpless? As if you were a pawn moved by invisible hands in a cruel and meaningless game."

"Yes, it does seem we don't really have much to say about it."

"Sam, you've got something to say about it, and you've got to keep on saying it—even if I have to leave you, and it looks as if I'm going to have to. We can't both live off the shop, and I don't seem to be able to manage enough bookings to pay our way. You've got about six hundred dollars' worth of engagements ahead. Just use that money to keep going. Someday you'll get a break. But no matter what happens you've got to keep on telling your story and doing your little part to make people love democracy and hate tyranny of every kind, big and little, more than ever before."

So Harold went back to the ministry. I hated to see him go, but I couldn't have asked for more: he had given better than a year of his life getting me started, and I felt deeply grateful.

That summer everybody was reading the news of Mussolini's campaign in Ethiopia. What did it all mean? In his melodramatic speeches from the Palazzo Venezia the Italian dictator had reviled the putrid corpse of liberty, extolled the manliness of war, and proclaimed fascism the coming order of society. Was the attack on Ethiopia the first skirmish in a war for the world, or was it merely the conquest of wha Mussolini considered a legitimate Italian claim?

If Mussolini succeeded in making the Mediterranean an Italian lake, as some believed was his intention, then wha would happen to the British Empire with Suez at the mercy of a self-styled enemy of democracy? If the British Empire broke up and fell into the hands of the Fascists, could America maintain an island of liberty in the Western

Hemisphere strong and self-sufficient enough to withstand the pressures of the predicted totalitarian age? How remote and speculative those questions were in those days! For most Americans, as for me, events had not yet fallen into that merciless march toward Armageddon which they were to assume later.

Besides reading and listening to the news and hobnobbing with other lecturers that summer, I attended evening lectures at the University of Chicago and occasionally dropped in on Bug House Square to hear the radicals and heretics let off steam. All in all, in spite of my impatience with an insolvent lecture career, it was a profitable summer, with many contacts to broaden and deepen my thinking.

Just before the summer ended, I lost my car because I couldn't keep up the payments. I hitchhiked from engagement to engagement until I had enough to buy another poverty liner, as Harold called them; then I disposed of my shop and went East. The next three years I spent digesting the news, lecturing to Americans about America, and traveling all over the eastern half of the United States—Chicago, St. Louis, Kansas City, Charleston, Pittsburgh, Philadelphia, Fort Worth, Dallas, Austin, Utica, Albany, Schenectady, Washington, New York.

Often nothing but the harrowing drift of events and the infectious enthusiasm of my audiences kept me going, for I was still barely meeting expenses. Everywhere I found the same cordial response, the same inspiration and encouragement. Lawyers, doctors, businessmen, teachers, workers, all of them overwhelmed me with honors and praises which I neither deserved nor quite understood. I told Harold once that the more miserable I made my story, the more they enjoyed it. On and on I went, shuttling back and forth across the country, sometimes driving a thousand miles at a stretch, fighting wind and ice and snow and rain and sleet, car trouble and the common cold to meet that next date, and always I felt more than amply rewarded by the appreciation of the people.

Perhaps no response was as complete and wholehearted as that of the teachers and educators in our public schools and colleges. To a group of teachers in Illinois, Dr. Melby, head of the department of education of Northwestern University, said, "With your permission I am going to yield my time to Mr. Rizk. You can always hear me, but this may be your last opportunity and privilege to hear him."

"With or without your permission," said Dr. Florence Hale, editor of the *Grade Teacher*, "I am going to tell your story on my radio hour next Saturday morning." And she did—with permission.

And with every new high-school or college audience, my faith in America increased. Once I had not been so sure of our immunity from the foreign "isms." But now, when I saw with my own eyes and heard with my own ears what pleased American audiences and what displeased them, when I saw how avidly the youth ate up every word of my story and message, when I saw how eagerly they responded to the challenge to live for America instead of off of it, when I saw the strength and beauty of their faces as I told them that the very problems we complain so much about are our greatest opportunities, I could no longer entertain any doubts about the soundness of my country's heart or any uncertainties of her future.

Even when I met the chronic grumblers who bristled with grievances as a Texas cactus bristles with spines, I regarded that as a healthy sign. In Germany, I thought, even honest discontent cannot be uttered without fear of firing squads and concentration camps. And if people cannot tell the truth about their own plight, their last hope of remedy has been removed. Not only are their lips sealed, but even the very hope of life itself.

Three years after pulling up stakes in Chicago, I was invited to address a meeting of the New York City Advertising Club. For several reasons I looked forward to this engagement with fear and trembling. First, my audience would be made up of top-notch executives, and naturally I felt uneasy. Secondly, I had been talking regularly for so long that my story was going stale. And thirdly, Lowell Thomas, the chairman, had invited some special guests, among them members of the staff of the *Reader's Digest*. At the last minute, however, something happened which removed all these anxieties in an instant. That very day Hitler invaded Czechoslovakia. I was overwhelmed with such a powerful surge of feeling and inspired with so many thoughts I could have addressed a parliament of men without a tremor.

Most ironically, on the same program that day was an Englishman just arrived in America who used all his time and half of mine telling us how much mightier was the umbrella than the sword. After Lowell Thomas succeeded in subduing him, I had left only sixteen minutes of an allotted half-hour. At the end of that time, however, the clamor for me to continue was so great that I went on until I had expressed all of my feelings. "Jemal Pasha, who ruled Turkey when I was a boy," I said, "was degenerate. But he was not degenerate enough to call his terrors, persecutions, and murders a 'new order.' Jemal Pasha was deceitful and perverted, but not deceitful and perverted enough to call his invasions and brutal conquests a 'mission of peace.' After seeing what the Nazis have done and are doing in Europe, I can forgive the Turks. They didn't know any better. But here are men reared in the Christian tradition who, with cold, deliberate calculation, pervert the truth, malign justice, and destroy mankind's faith in one of life's most sacred obligations—the obligation of the pledged word."

After the meeting one of the editors of the *Reader's Digest* (who, I learned later, administered American Near East Relief after the last war) spoke to me and invited me to his home. There one of the most enjoyable evenings of a lifetime reached an astonishing climax when my host said, "Salom, how would you like to lecture to the high-school boys and girls of America under the auspices of the *Reader's Digest?*"

"Why—why, nothing could make me happier."

"Perhaps," he said, "we can arrange it. You must understand, of course, that I can promise nothing, but if we feel satisfied that telling your story is really helping along the cause of good Americanism, there's a chance that we'll be interested in sponsoring you."

I tried hard to look calm, but actually I was so elated I could have jumped through the ceiling. The first chance I got I wrote to Harold. I told him that The Reader's Digest Association was interested in sponsoring me, paying my salary and expenses, and offering me to high schools and colleges as a public service. He wrote back and said, "I knew it all the time, Sime. I knew it all the time."

But I didn't know it all the time. Besides, the matter wasn't settled yet. It was to be arranged for me to speak in a selected group of schools for one month, and at the end of that time, if my work was satisfactory, I was to get a contract for one year. It seems to me now that there was as much hope and fear and anxiety crowded into that one month as into all of the five years I had waited for my American passport in Syria. For here was the richest, most inspiring opportunity America had afforded me—the opportunity to realize more fully the ambition an imaginative newspaperman had planted in me almost ten years before—the ambition to become a life servant of the country where I had found life so good.

CHAPTER XXII

Two Syrian-Americans

THE TRIAL MONTH OF LECTURING in the high schools was a success, and the *Reader's Digest* became my sponsor for one year; after that, another year; and then another.

I had already traveled a great deal in America and met many different kinds of people, but in the next three years I was to visit nearly every state in the Union. Freed of the tedious, time-consuming business of building an itinerary out of the scattered towns and cities of the United States, I now had, for the first time since quitting the shoe-repairing business, time and leisure to see, understand, and appreciate to the full the people and the places along the way.

And where are the people and where are the places I have not had the privilege of visiting in this vast country? What big city haven't I been lost in, or had a parking problem in? What little one-gas-station village haven't I passed through and wondered about? What great factory mill or mine haven't I toured, marveling at the ingenuity and the skill which created and operated such vast and throbbing enterprises? What famous parks, national shrines, or inspiring landscapes have I not gazed upon and gaped at? What monuments, cathedrals, and famous public buildings have I not stood before, filled with reverence and awe? The soft, kind contours of Pennsylvania's hills, the tumbled chaos of California's Sierras, the snow-streaked heads of mountains like Shasta and Rainier, the broad, rich valleys of rivers like the Mississippi and Missouri, the long, lonely deserts, the tenderly cultivated fields and orchards, the vineyards and pastures—from ocean to ocean and border to border I have seen America, big, broad, breathless. I have felt the throb of its power, the thrill of its vastness, the pull of its dream, and I have loved it. What day, indeed, has ever passed that I have not exclaimed, "What a country! What a country!"

And I have seen democracy at work in every corner of the land. I have seen something of its successes and failures; something of the huge and knotty problems which cry for answers, and something of the splendid people whose words, spirits, and deeds are rising to answer the cry. The more I saw and learned of our beautiful heritage and marvelous resources, the more I felt that, if we became discouraged in the face of our problems and began to look for a strong man to hand them to, we had no right to blame the people of Europe for turning to dictators. I felt that if

America could not solve her social problems democratically, then we could not expect any other nation in the world to do so.

Now and then I met people who were discouraged about democracy. They said, "Democracy is a failure. It is too slow, too clumsy to cope with the problems of these times. The parliamentary system belongs to the horse-and-buggy age. What we need now is a strong, streamlined government which can move swiftly and powerfully enough not only to keep up with our problems but to keep ahead of them. That means a government with a strong head who can make quick decisions and enforce them. When floods are sweeping down your valley you don't stop to call a meeting of the debating society for next Tuesday night."

Their complaint sounded plausible, but to such people I said, "You say democracy is a failure, because here and there it has failed. But what about the dictatorships? Aren't all their boasted successes really miserable and tragic failures? Do you call persecution a success merely because you can get away with it? Do you call murder a success because it has been made the special privilege of the government? Do you call lies a success simply because you can get a whole nation of people to believe them? Isn't it the real truth that the more any crime succeeds, the more it fails, because crime, persecution, murder, and lying are themselves symptoms of human failure, and because they inevitably boomerang against those who use them? And what about racial arrogance, national pride, regimentation, militarism, and all the other evils which the dictators have glorified into virtues?"

"You don't understand," they would say. "Those are the things the dictators have to do to revise the Versailles Treaty, abolish unemployment, and dissolve social unrest."

"Do you call taking men out of the bread line and putting them into the firing line solving unemployment? Isn't that an even greater failure than unemployment?"

"It is you who don't understand," they would say. "To meet life today, a nation has to have total conscription of all its man power, and military conscription is only part of the program. It's a way of achieving national unity."

"Is unity achieved with concentration camps and castor oil, purges and pogroms, real unity?" I would ask, and add, "To my mind the worst failure of human society is uniformity, running all individuals into the same mold, and the dictators have made that failure their goal. They actually boast about it. They boast that they've destroyed all political parties but one, that they've destroyed all labor unions, and that they will destroy all the churches. I'll grant that democracy hasn't succeeded one hundred per cent, but the dictators actually are working overtime trying to fail one hundred per cent."

"Oh, you're old-fashioned," they would say.

"You mean I *was* old-fashioned. When I lived under the Turkish regime in the old country and took for granted that that was the way the common people lived everywhere, I was old-fashioned. But when I came to America, I found something new. Give the people as much time ruling themselves as the tyrants have had misruling them, before you say democracy has failed."

But some people had grumbled about democracy so long that it had become a settled habit. You couldn't talk them out of it. So, as a parting shot, I would say, "Sometimes I think that the real trouble with democracy is that it has succeeded too well." And when they wanted to know what that meant, I would tell them about the following experience:

In 1939 I was entertained in the home of a wealthy Syrian-American who is also a leading politician in one of our states. When he arrived in New York from Syria after the last war, he was penniless, but very ambitious and energetic. Within a short time he had set his feet on the road to riches. And to improve his fortune he became a citizen and entered politics, backstage.

His home and the beautiful grounds surrounding it, he proudly boasted, cost him over $200,000. His children were attending private or parochial schools and enjoying all the luxuries and privileges money can buy.

During dinner our conversation got around to politics and inevitably to Roosevelt and Hitler and the policies of the two leaders.

We had not talked long before I was appalled by his bald, cynical disregard for everything my experience in America had taught me to consider sacred. He advocated denying the elementary rights of citizenship to the Jews and to other "inferior groups," forgetting that the vicious lies he was now repeating against the Jews were the very same lies that had been hurled against the Christians in Syria. My host applauded Hitler's handling of the Jewish question and saw nothing dangerous or inhuman in Hitler's New Order. He could not speak of our President without venom and profanity.

To my host politics was a game in which he exploited dopes and saps. He showed me two medals bestowed upon him for meritorious service by the Democratic party, yet he was without loyalty. His whole attitude was one of contempt for his party and the electorate because, as he put it, they were "nothing but a bunch of suckers."

He scoffed at the "naïve" belief of the people in him and in his promises. To him the generous characteristics of the American people, which made it easy for him to succeed, were nothing but stupid gullibility.

Here was a man who had a thousand times more reason

to love America than I had. The United States had given him wealth, success, prestige, power, opportunity for his children—all things he never could have found in the old country. And yet he was repaying America's hospitality by bringing organized intolerance from the old country and exploiting it in this new land that had given him refuge. I am thankful to say that he was the most ungrateful immigrant I ever met.

That's what I mean when I say that sometimes I think democracy has succeeded too well. It has made success possible to people who do not deserve it. They found freedom here and thought it was only a tool to fulfill their own selfish desires. They used, or rather abused, freedom to achieve power, and now they want to use their power to destroy that freedom.

Instead of dedicating their success to the common welfare, as every great American has always done, they have used it to fool the people and thwart their desires. It is hard to see any real difference between that Jew-hating politician and his kind on the one hand and the Nazis on the other. Both have a genuine contempt for the people, both use them for their selfish ends, and both have such twisted minds that they cannot recognize in themselves the vices which they presume to find and hate in others.

What a contrast to this man is another Syrian-American

whom I met recently, Dr. Michael Shadid, who pioneered the first co-operative hospital in the United States at Elk City, Oklahoma. American democracy gave Dr. Shadid a chance to succeed, too, but he has made his success serve the people, not exploit them.

Dr. Shadid had come to America before the turn of the century to finish a medical education begun at the American University at Beirut. But he had borrowed money to get here, so he peddled jewelry for two years to repay the loan. His success as a door-to-door salesman might have sidetracked him from his main interest but for the fact that one day he landed in a Texas college town and the sight of the campus stirred again his dream of becoming a doctor. He went back to school. Graduating from medical college, he set up practice in Missouri, later moving to Oklahoma. After twenty years as a country doctor, he began to think of taking things a little easier and chose Elk City as the best town in which to do it.

But then his real work began. He had always had two ambitions, one to heal the sick and the other to do something for the country which had given him so many opportunities. One problem which had early attracted his attention was, how to make better medical care available to people with low incomes. He had read with deep interest Dr. Ray Lyman Wilbur's report on the cost of medical care, which stated that half the illness in the country occurred among people earning twelve hundred dollars a year or less. He knew how difficult it was to provide a family with proper food on such an income, let alone careful medical examinations, costly operations, and hospitalization.

In and around Elk City were a lot of families trying to live on less than twelve hundred dollars a year. Dr. Shadid decided to do something about it, and the result was the first co-operative hospital in the United States—a hospital owned by the people it serves. In Elk City a family of four can get its medical care for $25 a year, with small, extra charges for hospitalization (two dollars per day), X-ray, anesthesia, drugs, etc.

"When I was peddling jewelry from door to door those first years in America," Dr. Shadid told me, "I saw a lot of America. And the more I saw of it, the more I loved it. But some things disturbed me. Here and there were injustice, oppression, and discrimination. I knew they didn't belong here. They were un-American. They didn't fit into the picture I had of this country. But there they were. Farmers paying outrageous interest rates and losing their farms, workers being overworked and underpaid, thousands of children denied their full educational opportunity, and hundreds of families not getting proper medical care. Of course, things were improving right along. I met people who were busy making this country, already the best in the world, even better. I decided I ought to do my share. I owed a debt to America for the opportunities she had given me, and I felt I ought to repay it in some concrete way. This hospital is part of my payment. Let's say it's the down payment."

"I have met a lot of Americans," I said, "who have asked if I knew you. From the wonderful things they have said about this hospital I am sure they'd be glad to give you a receipt marked 'Paid in full.'"

There are a lot of people like Dr. Shadid in this country. Some trace their ancestors through Plymouth Rock and some through Ellis Island. But regardless of origin, they are working quietly, obscurely, and unstintingly to give democracy the victory in one area of life after another, to extend it out to the very last frontier of human aspiration. They are the people who regard every problem as an opportunity. When you meet them and feel their deep, determined resolve, you know that the other kind of people can never defeat the American dream. You can't beat the people who built and are still building this America.